Contemporary's

Number Power

a real world approach to math

Ellen C. Frechette

McGraw Hill **Wright Group**

Wright Group

ISBN: 0-8092-2384-8

Send all inquiries to:
Wright Group/McGraw-Hill
130 E. Randolph, Suite 400
Chicago, IL 60601

Printed in the United States of America.

10 11 12 13 14 15   11 10 09

The **McGraw·Hill** Companies

Acknowledgements

(graph) "Percent of People Who Get Angry." *Almanac of the American People,* © 1988 by Tom and Nancy Biracree.

(chart) "How Salty Snacks Stack Up." © 1991 by Consumers Union of U.S., Inc. Yonkers, NY 10703-1057, a nonprofit organization. Reprinted with permission from the June 1991 issue of *Consumer Reports* for educational purposes only. No commercial use or photocopying permitted. To subscribe, call 1-800-234-1645 or visit at www.ConsumerReports.org.

(pictograph) "Professional Bowling Association Leading Money Winners." *The World Almanac and Book of Facts, 1999.*

(circle graph) "Origin of Foreign Students." Institute of International Education." Copyright 1991 by *USA Today.* Reprinted with permission.

(bar graph) "Number of Books in Print." R. R. Bowker's *Books in Print.*

Table of Contents

To the Student   vii

Analyzing Data Pretest   1

BUILDING NUMBER POWER   7

Understanding Data

Defining Data   8
Making Statements About Data   11
What Are Statistics?   13
Comparing Numbers   16
How Big Is a Billion?   19
Numbers vs. Rates   22
Group Project: Collecting Data   26

Organizing Data

Tables and Charts   28
Bar Graphs   32
Double Bar Graphs   36
Line Graphs   38
More Line Graphs   40
Visual Statistics   43
Pictographs   44
Circle Graphs   46
Line Plots   49
Scatter Diagrams   52
Arithmetic Mean   54
Median   56
Mode   57
Mean, Median, and Mode   58

Critical Thinking with Data   59

Group Project: Organizing Data   60

Analyzing Data

The Purpose of a Graph or Chart   62

Reading Data: Be Specific   67

Reading Data: Using Only the Information Given   70

The Language of Estimation   73

Accurate Estimating   75

Using More than One Data Source   78

Putting Data in Different Forms   81

Seeing Trends/Making Predictions   86

Group Project: Summarizing Your Data   90

Using Probability and Statistics

What Are the Chances?   92

Probabilities Between 1 and 0   94

Using Data to Estimate Probability   96

An Introduction to Sampling   99

Random Samples   102

An Introduction to Surveys   105

Margin of Error   109

Group Project: Write Your Own Survey   112

Evaluating Data

Do Statistics Lie?   114

Drawing Conclusions from Data   116

Misinterpreting Graphs   120

The Importance of Zero on a Scale   124

Understanding Correlation   127

Bias in Surveys and Statistics   132

Critical Thinking with Data   138

Group Project: A Closer Look at Surveys   142

Posttest A   144

Posttest B   155

USING NUMBER POWER 167

A Look at the U.S. Census 168

Are You Average? 170

Writing a Newspaper Article 172

A Look at Political Polling in History 174

Numbers in Advertising 176

Answer Key 178

Using a Calculator 190

Using Mental Math 191

Using Estimation 192

Measurements 193

Glossary 194

Index 197

To the Student

Do the following statistics sound familiar?

- There's a 40% chance of rain.
- The unemployment rate is 4%.
- 3 out of 4 people prefer brand X.
- $3 million will be added to the district education budget.

Welcome to *Number Power 8: Analyzing Data.* With this book, you will learn the language of data and statistics so that you can analyze and understand the numbers around you. This understanding will help you feel more comfortable and knowledgeable when faced with statistics.

Begin to pay more attention to the numbers around you. Find some statistics in a newspaper article or editorial. Think about how you might interpret them *differently.* Remember that although numbers may be based on facts, the statements made about them are not always accurate. *Analyzing Data* will help you understand how to interpret data and how to judge other people's interpretations.

The first part of the book, Building Number Power, contains five chapters giving you step-by-step instruction and practice with various kinds of data and statistics. The second part of the book, Using Number Power, gives you a chance to apply and extend the data analysis skills you have just learned.

Included in the back of this book are useful resources to make your work with numbers easier and smarter. Refer to the pages about using a calculator, using mental math, and estimating for quick, helpful explanations. You are reminded to use these skills throughout the book when you see the following icons:

 calculator icon

 mental math icon

estimation icon

As you work through *Analyzing Data,* check your answers with the answer key at the back of the book. A chart inside the back cover will help you keep track of your scores.

Analyzing Data Pretest

This test will tell you which sections of *Number Power 8* you need to concentrate on. Do every problem that you can. Correct answers are listed by page number at the back of the book. After you check your answers, the chart at the end of the test will guide you to the pages of the book where you need work.

For problems 1–4, refer to the following data.

State	1999 Population (to the nearest million)
Alabama	4,000,000
Arkansas	3,000,000
California	32,000,000
Idaho	1,000,000
Pennsylvania	12,000,000

1. Which of the states listed has the largest population?

   a. Idaho
   b. California
   c. Pennsylvania

2. Complete the following sentence.

   The table above shows the 1999 _____ to the nearest million for five states.

3. Write a sentence that compares the population of Arkansas to the population of Alabama.

4. How many more people lived in California than in Alabama in 1999?

   a. 32,000,000
   b. 30,000,000
   c. 28,000,000

For problems 5–8, refer to the following data.

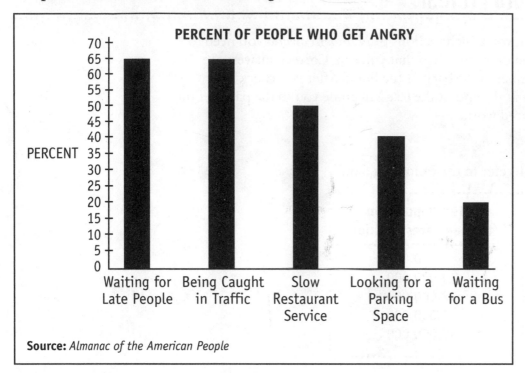

PERCENT OF PEOPLE WHO GET ANGRY

Source: *Almanac of the American People*

5. Approximately what percent of people get angry looking for a
    parking space?

    a. 40%
    b. 50%
    c. 55%

6. Which activity made more people angry: being caught in traffic or
    waiting for a bus?

7. Write a statement about the percent of people who get angry at
    slow restaurant service.

8. Find the mean (average) percent of people who get angry in the five
    situations on the graph.

For problems 9–12, refer to the following data.

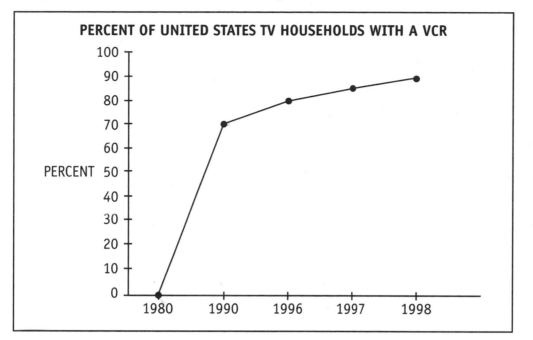

PERCENT OF UNITED STATES TV HOUSEHOLDS WITH A VCR

9. Approximately what percent of TV households in the United States had a VCR in 1997?

   a. 80%
   b. 85%
   c. 90%

10. Estimate and compare the percent of U.S. TV households with VCRs in 1980 and 1990.

    In 1990, approximately _____ times as many U.S. households had VCRs as in 1980.

    a. one-seventh
    b. three
    c. seven

11. If the trend continues, what percent of TV households in the United States will have a VCR by the year 2000?

    a. less than 90%
    b. about 90%
    c. more than 90%

12. Which of these statements is *not* based on the graph?

    a. More people in the U.S. had a VCR in 1998 than in 1997.
    b. People rented more videotapes in 1998 than in 1997.
    c. More than $\frac{2}{3}$ of all TV households in the U.S. had a VCR in 1996.

For problems 13–15, refer to the following data.

According to the U.S. Department of Housing and Urban Development, 45% of homeless people in 1998 were families. Single men made up 43% of the homeless population, and 12% of the homeless were single women. These statistics provide more evidence of the changing face of America's homeless.

13. Complete the circle graph below. Be sure to include all labels and numbers for each section of the graph.

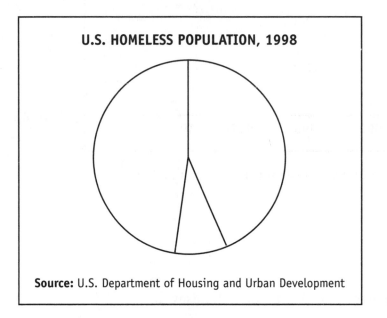

U.S. HOMELESS POPULATION, 1998

Source: U.S. Department of Housing and Urban Development

14. If a city counted 1,200 homeless people, how many of them would be single women?

   a. 144
   b. 480
   c. 1,000

15. Write a statement that compares two sections on the circle graph.

For problems 16–17, refer to the following situation.

The cards at the right are lying facedown on a table.

16. Suppose you pick up one card. What is the probability that the card you chose is a multiple of 2?

    a. 1 out of 2
    b. 2 out of 3
    c. 3 out of 5

17. What is the probability of choosing a 5 from these cards?

    a. 0
    b. $\frac{1}{2}$
    c. 1

For problem 18, refer to the following information.

A year 2000 survey indicated that most Americans consider themselves to be overweight. A total of 80% of people surveyed feel that they should lose at least 10 pounds. These figures show an increase from previous years. In 1970, for example, 59% of people surveyed felt that they were 10 pounds overweight. In 1980, the figure rose to 72%. And in 1990, the figure was 78%.

18. Use the data above to finish constructing the line graph below. Be sure to include a title, labels on both axes, and the data line connecting the plotted points.

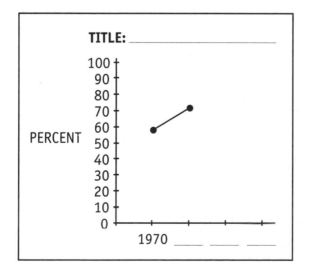

For problem 19, refer to the following scatter diagram.

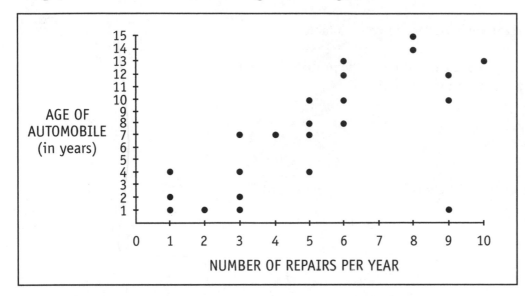

19. Write a statement comparing the age of automobiles and the number of repairs per year.

Analyzing Data Pretest Chart

If you miss more than one problem in any section of this test, you should complete the lessons on the practice pages indicated on this chart. If you miss no problems in a section of this test, you may not need further study in that chapter. However, to master data analysis, we recommend that you work through the entire book. As you do, focus on the skills covered in each chapter.

PROBLEM NUMBERS	SKILL AREA	PRACTICE PAGES
1, 2, 4	tables and charts	28–31
3, 7, 15	making statements about data	11–12
5, 6	bar graphs	32–37
8	mean, median, and mode	54–58
9, 18	line graphs	38–42
10	estimation	73–77
11	seeing trends	86–89
12	using only the information given	70–72
13, 14	circle graphs	46–48
16, 17	probability	92–98
19	understanding correlation	127–131

Building
Number
Power

UNDERSTANDING DATA

Defining Data

Let's start our discussion of data with questions about you.
* What is your age?
* How many people are in your immediate family?
* How many people are living in your home?
* How many languages do you speak?
* How many times per week do you read the newspaper?
* How many different sports do you watch regularly on TV?

The numbers you gave in answer to the questions above represent **data.** *Data* refers to a collection of numbers that gives information about a subject—in this case, you!

Here are some examples of data that are common in everyday life. Put a check next to any you are familiar with.

The nutrition label on a cereal box gives data on calories, fat content, vitamins, and sodium.

NUTRITION INFORMATION		
CALORIES		160
PROTEIN, g		4
CARBOHYDRATE, g		33
FAT, TOTAL, g		3
UNSATURATED, g	3	
SATURATED, g	0	
CHOLESTEROL, mg		0
SODIUM, mg		40
POTASSIUM, mg		125

A graph in a newspaper displays population data.

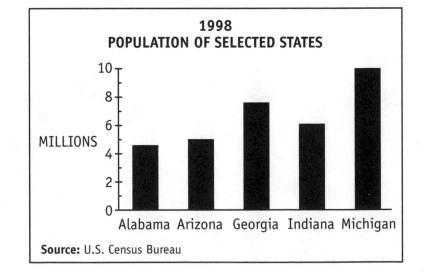

1998 POPULATION OF SELECTED STATES

MILLIONS

Source: U.S. Census Bureau

A document for factory employees contains data about the sizes of certain manufactured items.

Identification Number	Size
1A714	12 mm
1A820	14 mm
2B640	20 mm
2B724	26 mm
3C438	30 mm

A recent survey of Rand County residents conducted by Environment Aware, Inc., revealed that, of those surveyed,

- 47% buy and use recycled products

- 90% would buy more recycled products if the prices were lower

- 76% have trouble finding recycled products

An article in a magazine provides data concerning the use of recycled products. People use data all the time to analyze situations and make decisions. Chances are that you are familiar with at least one of these examples of data.

Gathering Data

Where do we get data? How is it collected? Depending on the subject, data can be gathered in many different ways. For example,

- A scientist might collect data by measuring the quantities of chemicals in a series of test tubes.

- A teacher might collect data about test scores by keeping a record of all test and quiz grades given in a class.

- An environmental worker might gather data by observing and recording what kinds of animals and birds live in a certain region.

- A government worker might collect data by analyzing questionnaires filled out by citizens.

In fact, you may not realize it, but various types of data are being collected around you every day. If you have ever filled out a census form or responded to a telephone survey, you have supplied data that some person or organization is collecting.

Check off any of the forms of data collection that you have participated in.

questionnaire
consumer product survey
credit or job application form
U.S. Census form
opinion poll
voting
other (What was it?_____)

· ·

To get a better feel for data, collect your own data in this activity.

Choose a street corner near where you live and record information about the first 10 people you see, using the chart below. Or, observe the first 10 characters you see on a TV program. To record the data when you see a person, put a slash, or **tally mark** (|), in the columns that apply. Tally marks help you "see the numbers."

(**Hint:** When you have recorded four tally marks in a row, your *fifth* mark should be a slash through the four marks, like this:

॥Ⅱ

This tallying method makes it easier to count up your marks later.)

For example, if the first person you saw was a frowning man wearing glasses and carrying a shopping bag, your chart would look like this:

Male	Female	Wearing Glasses	Not Wearing Glasses	Smiling	Not Smiling	Carrying Something	Not Carrying Anything
|		|			|	|	

Making Statements About Data

Fall 1998 Enrollment in Full-Time Day Schools

State	Pupils per Teacher	Teachers' Average Pay
Alabama	16.6	$32,818
Alaska	17.5	$51,738
California	22.9	$43,725
New Jersey	13.6	$50,442

Source: National Center for Education Statistics

Write a short statement using the data in the chart. There is no single correct answer, so feel free to be creative. The first one is started for you.

1. California has _____

_____

2. _____

_____

What can be said about the information in the chart? Here are some statements you might have written about the data in the chart.

- California has more pupils per teacher than Alabama.

- Of the four states listed, Alaska has the highest average teacher's pay.

- Alabama teachers have the lowest average pay of the four states listed, but not the fewest pupils per teacher.

- Teachers' salaries vary from state to state.

Some of these statements refer to specific pieces of information in the data.

EXAMPLE　California has more pupils per teacher than Alabama.

Other statements make a more general comment about the data.

EXAMPLE　Teachers' salaries vary from state to state.

The one thing that these statements have in common is that they all say something *true* about the data.

Throughout this book, you will be looking at different types of data and making statements about them. Don't worry if you had trouble coming up with a statement about the data in the table. You will get plenty of practice. By the end of this book, you will be able to *interpret and write statements* about almost any data you come across in school, at work, or in a newspaper or magazine.

IMPORTANT!
Whenever you make a statement about data, be sure to write a **complete sentence.** The phrase *seventeen pupils per teacher* does not have any meaning. However, *Alaska averaged about seventeen pupils per teacher in 1998* does have meaning.

Practice writing statements about the data you collected on page 10. The questions below should help you get started. Remember that you can be as straightforward or creative as you like when writing your statements. Be sure that each statement is a complete sentence and is true according to the data you collected.

Below are some questions to help you get started.

- Out of 10 people, how many were female?
- Did you see more people with glasses or without?
- How many people were carrying something?
- Who was smiling more often—men or women?
- Did more men than women wear glasses?

Statement 1: _____

_____

Statement 2: _____

_____

Statement 3: _____

_____

Statement 4: _____

_____

Statement 5: _____

_____

What Are Statistics?

Of the 4,280 people who responded to our magazine's survey, 71% said that the government should provide subsidized child care for all workers. Twenty percent stated that child care is not the government's concern, and 9% had no opinion on the issue.

What numbers appear in this article?
Have you read articles similar to this?
How do these numbers differ from the data you saw earlier?

Many statements you read in newspapers and magazines or hear on the radio or television contain **statistics** such as those in the article above. The term *statistics* refers to the collection, organization, and interpretation of data.

For example, on page 10, you collected data about a group of people. If you organized and interpreted this information, you might use statistics to help present the facts.

Imagine what the article above would sound like if it simply listed the information obtained from the survey.

QUESTION: Do you think that the government should provide subsidized child care for all workers?

Miriam Brown from Spokane, WA, responded yes.
Carlos Young from Cairo, IL, responded yes.
David Antony from Los Angeles, CA, responded no.
Walter Fireton from Baton Rouge, LA, responded yes.
Vera Roundtree from Orono, ME, responded no.
Mary Caviness from Kansas City, MO, had no opinion.
Maureen Burns from Windham, NH, responded yes.

As you can see, an article that listed each person's opinion would be extremely long. And it would be practically impossible to understand the results of the survey. Instead, the writer **summarizes** the data by using percents.

71% said "yes."

20% said "no."

9% said "no opinion."

Using tally marks, record the responses given on page 13 to help you "see the numbers." Miriam Brown's response has already been recorded.

Yes	No	No Opinion
|		

How Are Statistics Presented?

Once a group of data is collected, the numbers are counted and put into a form that is easy for people to understand.

In the example on page 13, the magazine probably issued a questionnaire or did a phone survey to determine what people thought about government-subsidized child care.

- What different ways can you think of to organize the information?

- How did the magazine present its data?

> **Math Recap**
> Data can be represented by **percents.** Remember that *percent* means "out of one hundred."

The statement that 71% think government should provide child care means that 71 out of every 100 people surveyed think government should provide child care.

The magazine received 4,280 responses to its survey. It chose to represent its data as *percents*. What other methods could it have used?

1. The magazine could have *listed* each individual's response separately, as you saw on page 13. This is a long and awkward method.

2. The magazine could have given *numbers* instead of percents.

   "Out of 4,280 responses, 856 people did not like the idea of government-subsidized child care."

3. The magazine also could have used *fractions*.

   "Approximately $\frac{7}{10}$ of respondents favored government-subsidized child care."

4. *Ratios* are another way to present data. You may be familiar with this technique in advertisements.

   "7 out of 10 (7:10) respondents favored government-subsidized child care."

   Ratios are most often written in fraction form: $\frac{7}{10}$.

Read the following lines taken from newspapers, magazines, and work reports. Express the numbers given as a percent, a fraction ratio, and a ratio.

EXAMPLE   "3 out of 10 students do not own a calculator."

<u>30%</u>   <u>$\frac{3}{10}$</u>   <u>3:10 or 30:100</u>

percent   fraction ratio   ratio

1. "Employees pass the physical exam 95 out of 100 times."

   _____   _____   _____

   percent   fraction ratio   ratio

2. "8 out of every 100 people in Newton are unemployed."

   _____   _____   _____

   percent   fraction ratio   ratio

3. "7 out of 10 customers prefer orange to grape juice."

   _____   _____   _____

   percent   fraction ratio   ratio

4. "Out of 200 questionnaires returned, 60 were completed by females."

   _____   _____   _____

   percent   fraction ratio   ratio

5. "The risk of mechanical error is 1 out of 100."

   _____   _____   _____

   percent   fraction ratio   ratio

6. "The ratio of computer users to non-users was 4 to 5."

   _____   _____   _____

   percent   fraction ratio   ratio

Comparing Numbers

- Your town government votes to give $80,000 to the parks and recreation department.

- You get an offer of $80,000 for your house.

- The legislature voted in favor of an $80,000 government-subsidized school lunch program.

Is 80,000 a large number or a small number?
How do you decide?

> One of the most important things to know about a number is this:
>
> A number is neither large nor small until you compare it to another number.

Let's look at the first example above. What other information would help you decide whether or not $80,000 is a lot of money for parks and recreation?

You might compare $80,000 to some of these numbers.

- **The amount of money allocated the previous year.** For example, if the town had allocated $200,000 last year, perhaps $80,000 does not seem like a very large figure.

- **The total amount of money in the town budget.** If the town had a budget of $125,000, then $80,000 would seem like a lot of money, given the fact that the town must also support schools, fire and police departments, maintenance work, and so forth.

- **The amount allotted to parks and recreation in similar neighboring towns.** If you compared $80,000 to the $10,000, $8,000, and $22,000 that three similar towns were spending, you would certainly think $80,000 was a lot of money.

When you see or hear a number, be careful not to make a judgment about its size until you have a chance to compare it to other related figures.

Which of the following numbers would be useful in determining whether the $80,000 offered for your house is a large or small number? Put a check mark next to the numbers that you would use to compare with the $80,000.

  a. the amount paid for a similar house in your neighborhood

  b. your neighbor's salary

  c. the number of houses on your street

  d. the price you paid for the house last year

You were right if you chose **a** and **d.** No matter how high or low your neighbor's salary is or how many houses there are in your neighborhood, these numbers will not tell you anything about the price of your house.

Now finish the following sentences.

- $80,000 for a house would be a *large* amount of money if

  _____.

- $80,000 for a house would be a *small* amount of money if

  _____.

Here are some sample sentences.

- $80,000 for a house would be a *large* amount of money if **I paid only $40,000 for it last year.**

- $80,000 for a house would be a *small* amount of money if **my neighbor sold the same kind of house for $100,000 two months ago.**

· ·

Make two statements about the $80,000 school lunch program.

1. $80,000 for the school lunch program would be a lot of money if

    _____

    _____

2. $80,000 for the school lunch program would be a small amount of money if _____

    _____

    _____

Don't rely on other people's interpretations of the size of numbers. It's important to draw your *own* conclusions about the information. A good start is to *compare* the information being presented to other amounts. To see how the same number can be looked on as both large and small, read the following excerpts from two different newscasts.

> Yesterday, a crowd of approximately 100 people marched in front of City Hall, protesting the pay raises the legislature had voted in on Tuesday. A handful of people held up signs supporting the increased salaries.

> Compared to last year's enormous protests over high salaries for government officials, the group of 100 or so protesters in front of City Hall yesterday was hardly noticed.

The *fact* is that 100 people stood outside City Hall. How you *interpret* this fact depends on what you compare the numbers to.

Look at the figures given below. What other numbers would be helpful in deciding whether these numbers are small or large?

EXAMPLE $100 to repair a stereo
It would be helpful to know *how much another place would charge for repairs.*

3. 400 people at a fund-raiser
    It would be helpful to know _____

    _____

4. 90 people laid off in a company
    It would be helpful to know _____

    _____

5. 3 guns confiscated in a police raid
    It would be helpful to know _____

    _____

6. $20 to purchase a painting
    It would be helpful to know _____

    _____

7. $2,000 to buy a car
    It would be helpful to know _____

    _____

How Big Is a Billion?

Ticket sales from the movie *Titanic* totaled $427 million in 1997.

The United States' federal debt (the amount by which government spending exceeded government income) in 1997 was $5.4 trillion.

Do you have a good understanding of the size of the numbers above?
When you read a very large number, what do you do to determine its size?

For many people, the bigger a number is, the less meaning it has. Let's review **place value** to help in our understanding of large numbers.

1	one
$1 \times 10 = 10$	ten
$10 \times 10 = 100$	one hundred
$100 \times 10 = 1,000$	one thousand
$1,000 \times 10 = 10,000$	ten thousand
$10,000 \times 10 = 100,000$	one hundred thousand
$100,000 \times 10 = 1,000,000$	one million
$1,000,000 \times 10 = 10,000,000$	ten million
$10,000,000 \times 10 = 100,000,000$	one hundred million
$100,000,000 \times 10 = 1,000,000,000$	one billion

Express the values in word or numeral forms as needed.

EXAMPLES   30,000,000 *thirty million* _____

two trillion *2,000,000,000,000* _____

1. 900,000 _____

2. 8,000,000 _____

3. 90,000,000 _____

4. one hundred million _____

5. two billion _____

6. seven hundred thousand _____

Math Recap
To multiply a whole number by 10, add a zero at the right.

The function of zeros can help you understand the relative size of numbers.

EXAMPLE 1   One million is how many times greater than a hundred thousand?

STEP 1 Write each amount in numeral form. Put the lesser number on top.	100,000 1,000,000
STEP 2 Cross out one zero at a time in each number until there are no zeros left in the lesser number. Be sure to cross out the same number of zeros in each number.	100,0̸0̸0̸ 1,000,0̸0̸0̸
STEP 3 Count the number of zeros left in the larger number.	1,000,0̸0̸0̸ One zero is left.
STEP 4 Your knowledge of place value tells you that one zero represents 10.	

ANSWER: One million is 10 times greater than one hundred thousand.

EXAMPLE 2   How many times greater is one billion than one million?

three zeros ─────→ 1,000,0̸0̸0̸ ←── cross out
left   1,000,0̸0̸0̸,0̸0̸0̸ ←── six zeros

ANSWER: One billion equals one thousand times one million.

When you come across large numbers like these, you need to have a basic understanding of their *relative* size (size in relation to other numbers). There is a big difference in value between a million and a billion! To illustrate how big a difference, think about this:

- It takes $11\frac{1}{2}$ days for a million seconds to pass.

- It takes almost 32 years for a billion seconds to pass.

- If you had 5 million dollars, you could spend $10,000 a day for a year and still have more than a million dollars left.

Use the "times 10" chart on page 19 and the method shown on page 20 to fill in the following.

EXAMPLE   Almost 4 million Roman Catholics live in East Asia. Almost 400 million Roman Catholics live in Latin America.

There are _100_ times as many Roman Catholics in Latin America as in East Asia.

    4,000,000   4 million

    400,000,000   400 million
    ↗
    two zeros mean
    100 times

7. Approximately 160,000,000 Buddhists live in South Asia. About 160,000 Buddhists live in North America.

    There are _____ times as many Buddhists in South Asia as in North America.

8. An estimated 750,000,000 people in East Asia consider themselves atheist or nonreligious. An estimated 75,000,000 Europeans include themselves in this category.

    _____ times as many East Asians as Europeans consider themselves atheist or nonreligious.

9. About 100,000 Jews live in Oceania. About 1,000,000 Jews live in Latin America.

    There are _____ times as many Jews living in Latin America as in Oceania.

10. Approximately 1,500,000,000 Christians exist worldwide, compared to 15,000,000 Jews.

    There are approximately _____ times as many Christians as Jews worldwide.

11. About 90,000,000 Catholics live in Africa, out of a total of 900,000,000 Catholics worldwide.

    There are _____ times as many Catholics in the world as in Africa.

Numbers vs. Rates

Which of the highways in the chart at the right would you prefer to drive on? Why?

1999 Accident Report

Highway	Number of Accidents
A	110
B	75
D	10
G	90
HH	12
MM	170

Did you say that you would rather drive on *Highway D* because it had the fewest accidents and therefore was the safest to drive on?

You may have made the common mistake of confusing *numbers* with **rates.** Before you can decide which highway is the safest, you need to know some other numbers.

For example, would you change your mind if you knew that only 3,000 cars travel on Highway D per year, compared to 75,000 on Highway B?

The chart above really does not give you much useful information. What would be more helpful is to know how many accidents occurred per one hundred cars. In other words, you need to know the *rate* of accidents, not just the *number* of accidents.

Now look at the revised chart. Unlike the chart above, this chart gives enough information to determine the rate of accidents. Do you know how to determine the rates?

Highway	Number of Accidents	Total Number of Cars per Year
A	110	55,000
B	75	75,000
D	10	3,000
G	90	60,000
HH	12	8,000
MM	170	80,000

To figure out each rate, divide the number of accidents by the total number of cars.

Highway A: 110 ÷ 55,000 =

A calculator entry would be

The calculator displays

| 0.002 |

Change the decimal to a percent by moving the decimal point two places to the right.

0.002 = 0.2%

Now find the accident rates for the remaining highways.

Which highway has the lowest accident rate?

Highway

A	*0.002*	=	*0.2* %
B	_____	=	_____ %
D	_____	=	_____ %
G	_____	=	_____ %
HH	_____	=	_____ %
MM	_____	=	_____ %

Highway B, with a rate of 0.1%, is the safest. Although this highway had 75 accidents, its accident *rate* is relatively low considering that so many cars travel on it.

Remember: A rate gives you more information than a number does, because a rate is actually *two* numbers—a number *compared to* another number.

A percent is the rate most commonly used—it represents a number out of one hundred. For example, which statement below gives you more information?

Statement A   There are 6,400 people living below the poverty level in our town.

Statement B   In our town, 17% of the people live below the poverty level.

Both statements are true, but statement B is the only statement that gives you information about the *size* of the poverty problem. Unless you know the total number of residents, statement A does not tell you much. The number 6,400 could be a huge number (if residents totaled 12,000) or a relatively small number (if residents totaled 220,000).

Look at the information below, then make
- **two statements about numbers**
- **two statements about rates**
- **a statement comparing numbers vs. rates**

A survey organization asked the employees of five different companies in the metro area this question: "Are you satisfied with your company's health benefits?" The results are shown below.

Company	Satisfied Employees	Total Number of Employees	Rate of Satisfaction
Walton Company	190	1,000	_____
Kramer, Inc.	13	87	_____
Psytech	440	3,800	_____
Ranger, Intl.	90	450	_____
Horton & Co.	26	105	_____

Listed below are some questions to help you get started.

1. What company had the *least number* of satisfied employees, and what is that number?

   Statement: _____

   _____

2. What companies had the *greatest number* of satisfied employees?

   Statement: _____

   _____

3. What company had the *lowest rate* of satisfaction?

   Statement: _____

   _____

4. What company had the *highest rate* of satisfaction?

   Statement: _____

   _____

5. Compare the *highest number* of satisfied employees with that company's employee satisfaction *rate*.

   Statement: _____

   _____

One of the most common rates that you will find in the news is the **unemployment rate.** Instead of reporting exactly how many people are out of work, the government reports a rate.

A 6.9% unemployment rate, for example, means that 6.9 (almost 7) people out of every 100 people in the labor force are not working.

The government also provides statistics for different segments of the labor force. For example, in 1999, the unemployment rate for the entire labor force was 4.3%. However, among young people ages 16–19, the rate was 14%—over three times that rate!

Use the chart below to write three statements about the unemployment rates for various years and among various segments of the labor force.

U.S. Unemployment Rates

Year	Total Work Force	Both Sexes 16–19 Years	Caucasian	African American
1995	5.6%	17.5%	4.9%	10.4%
1996	5.4	16.8	4.8	10.5
1997	4.9	15.1	4.2	10.2
1998	4.5	14.3	3.9	9.2
1999	4.3	14.0	3.8	8.9

Source: Bureau of Labor Statistics

6. Compare the unemployment rate for the total work force in two different years.

_____

_____

7. Write a statement about unemployment among teenagers in the United States using the figures above.

_____

_____

8. Compare the unemployment rates of Caucasians to the rates of African Americans during one year.

_____

_____

Group Project: Collecting Data

Use the questionnaire below to collect data. The more people in your group collecting the data, the better.

- You may photocopy the questionnaire and have people fill it out themselves, or you may survey people directly by asking them the questions out loud and recording their responses.

- Try to get information from a variety of people—students, co-workers, friends, and some people whom you don't know well. Try to get a variety of ages and ancestry if possible.

- Keep the responses to your survey in a folder because you will be using the data you collected as you work through this book.

Questionnaire/Survey

Sex   M ☐   F ☐   Age ☐

Are you married?   Yes ☐   No ☐

Do you consider yourself more of a "day person" or a "night owl"? _____

What section of the newspaper do you read first? _____

Do you live alone?   Yes ☐   No ☐

How many hours of television do you watch per week? _____

Do you have a dog? ☐   a cat? ☐   a bird? ☐

Do you recycle any products?   Yes ☐   No ☐

If yes, paper? ☐   aluminum? ☐   glass? ☐

Are you satisfied with the current president?   Yes ☐   No ☐

Which are you more concerned about, the economy ☐ or the environment? ☐

Should Americans buy only products made in America?   Yes ☐   No ☐

How many close friends do you have, not including family? _____

How many times per week do you see people for a social occasion? _____

Count up the responses to your survey using the space below. First, use tally marks as you did on page 10. Then count up the tally marks and write a total at the end of each line.

Sex
Male: _____
Female: _____

Age
15–24: _____
25–34: _____
35–44: _____
45–54: _____
55–64: _____
65–74: _____
75–84: _____

Married
Yes: _____
No: _____

"Day Person" or "Night Owl"
Day: _____
Night: _____

Section of Newspaper (write in)
_____   _____
_____   _____
_____   _____

Living Alone
Yes: _____
No: _____

Hours of Television per Week
0–4: _____
5–8: _____
9–12: _____
13–16: _____
17–20: _____
Over 20: _____

Pets
Dog: _____
Cat: _____
Bird: _____

Recycling
Paper: _____
Aluminum: _____
Glass: _____

Satisfied with President
Yes: _____
No: _____

Biggest Concern
Economy: _____
Environment: _____

Buy American
Yes: _____
No: _____

Number of Close Friends
0–2: _____
3–5: _____
6–7: _____
8–9: _____
10 or more: _____

Social Occasions per Week
0–2: _____
3–5: _____
6–7: _____

ORGANIZING DATA

Tables and Charts

How Salty Snacks Stack Up (One-Ounce Serving)					
	Potato Chips	Pretzels	Popcorn*	Corn Chips	Peanuts
Calories	152	111	76	153	170
Fat	10 g	1 g	1 g	9 g	14 g
From Fat	60% of calories	8% of calories	12% of calories	53% of calories	74% of calories
Sodium	160 mg	451 mg	1 mg	218 mg	138 mg

*Air-popped corn. The microwave type has about twice the calories. It contains 9 grams of fat (that's 55 percent of its calories) and 196 milligrams of sodium.

Source: *Consumer Reports,* June 1991

Why are tables like the one above often used to display data? What does this table have in common with other charts you've seen?

Charts and tables are useful because they organize data in an easy-to-read format. Effective tables and charts have at least four elements.

- A **title** describes the subject of the table or chart.

- **Headings** (**column** and **row** labels) show what information will be provided in the table.

- **Data** (for example, the numbers listed under and next to the headings above) gives the most specific information in the table.

- The **source** is usually found in smaller print below a graph, table, or chart, and it tells where the data actually came from.

To find specific information in a table, you will need to read across a row and down a column to where the row and column intersect (meet).

EXAMPLE Look at the table on page 28. How much sodium is in one ounce of corn chips?

> **STEP 1** Find *Sodium* in the list of row headings at the left in the table.
>
> **STEP 2** Follow the row across until you come to the *Corn Chips* column, labeled at the top of the table.
>
> **STEP 3** The number at the intersection of the *sodium* row and the *Corn Chips* column is 218 mg.

ANSWER: There are **218 mg** of sodium in one ounce of corn chips.

....

Use the table on page 28 to fill in the blanks.

1. One ounce of air-popped popcorn contains _____ gram(s) of fat.

2. _____% of the calories in peanuts come from fat.

3. One ounce of microwave popcorn has about _____ calories.

Use the table to decide if each statement is true or false.

T   F   **4.** Corn chips have more calories than potato chips.

T   F   **5.** Popcorn has 4% more calories from fat than pretzels.

T   F   **6.** A bowl containing one ounce of corn chips and one ounce of pretzels contains more than 200 calories.

Make two statements using the data in the table. The first one has been started for you.

7. A one-ounce serving of peanuts _____

_____

8. _____

_____

9. **Critical Thinking** *Consumer Reports* is a magazine published by a nonprofit, independent organization. Do you think the information in its charts would be different from charts you might see in advertisements? Why?

Use the information given in this newspaper article to fill in the table below.

> **STEP 1** Read the article below.
>
> **STEP 2** Write a title for the table and fill in the source line.
>
> **STEP 3** Label the columns (*$50,000 or More* has been filled in) and rows (the *Bank Credit Card* row has been labeled).
>
> **STEP 4** Fill in the data (*94%* has been filled in).

According to *Money Express* magazine, 94% of Americans earning $50,000 or more had bank credit cards, and 54% had gasoline credit cards. Fourteen percent of this group had an Express Gold card. Of Americans earning $25,000–$34,999, 73% had a bank credit card, 33% had gasoline cards, and 3% had an Express Gold card. Finally, of Americans earning less than $15,000, only 36% had a bank card, and only 1% had an Express Gold card. However, 19% of this group had gasoline cards.

10. Title _____

	Income Level		
Type of Card	*$50,000 or more*		
Bank Credit Card	*94%*		

Source: _____

Use the table on page 30 to fill in the blanks.

11. _____% of Americans earning $25,000–$34,999 have a bank credit card.

12. 19% of Americans earning less than $15,000 have a _____ credit card.

13. 3% of Americans earning _____ have an Express Gold card.

14. _____% more Americans earning $50,000 or more have a bank credit card than a gasoline credit card.

Use the table to decide if each statement is true or false.

T F **15.** Of Americans earning $25,000–$34,999, 14% hold an Express Gold card.

T F **16.** Americans earning $50,000 or more are the highest percent of credit card holders for every card listed.

T F **17.** Less than 50% of Americans earning $25,000–$34,999 hold a bank credit card.

T F **18.** Of Americans earning less than $15,000, 1% hold an Express Gold card.

Make two statements using the data in the table. The first one has been started for you.

19. The bank credit card _____

_____

20. _____

_____

Bar Graphs

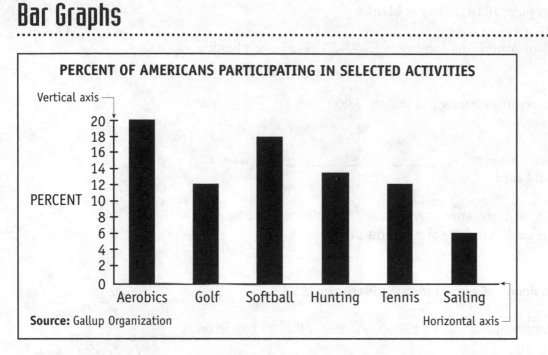

PERCENT OF AMERICANS PARTICIPATING IN SELECTED ACTIVITIES

Vertical axis

PERCENT

Aerobics Golf Softball Hunting Tennis Sailing

Source: Gallup Organization

Horizontal axis

**Have you ever seen a graph similar to this one?
What is being compared on the graph?**

How do you read a **bar graph** like the one above? Just as with a table or chart, you need to pay attention to the title and source line. Listed below are other major parts of a bar graph that will help you interpret the data.

- *The vertical axis, the horizontal axis, and their labels*

On the graph above, the **vertical axis** represents percent, while the **horizontal axis** shows different activities.

- *The bars*

Bars can be vertical (as in the graph above) or horizontal. Value is shown by the height or length of each bar. Each bar on the graph above represents a different activity; for example, aerobics or softball.

- *The scale and range*

A **scale** marks the length of each bar and is labeled in equal increasing values. The **range** is the lowest value on the graph through the highest. The scale on the graph above shows percents in increases of 2 with a range from 0 to 20.

You may already know how to read a bar graph.

EXAMPLE   What percent of Americans play golf?

>   **STEP 1**   Find the bar labeled *Golf* on the horizontal axis.
>
>   **STEP 2**   Move your finger from the top of the bar across to the corresponding value on the vertical axis. Or place the edge of a paper across the top of the bar to the vertical axis.
>
>   **STEP 3**   The value is 12.

ANSWER: The graph tells you that **12% of Americans play golf.**

Now figure out what percent of Americans play tennis. Can you see that the *Tennis* bar rises to a point between two points labeled on the scale?

The range of percents given on the graph is from 0% to 20%, and the values are labeled in multiples of two (2, 4, 6, 8, and so on).

The value between 10 and 12 is 11; therefore, **11% of Americans play tennis.**

· ·

Take a few minutes to determine from the graph on page 32 what percent of Americans participate in each of the activities listed.

1. Aerobics: _____

2   Softball: _____

3. Hunting: _____

4. Sailing: _____

Bar graphs are useful for more than just showing specific data. A quick look at a bar graph allows you to make comparisons very easily.

For example, do more Americans play softball or tennis?

All you need to do is compare the lengths of the two bars. The softball bar is taller than the tennis bar. Therefore, **more Americans play softball.**

5. **Critical Thinking**   How do you think the Gallup Organization got the data for this information? Did its staff ask every single American if he or she plays golf or tennis?

Now apply what you have just learned to another bar graph. Notice the similarities and differences between it and the one on page 32.

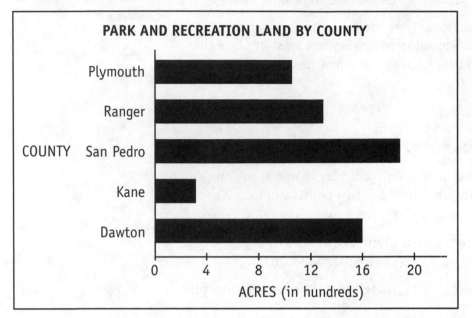

PARK AND RECREATION LAND BY COUNTY

6. What is the title of the graph?   Title: _____

7. What does the vertical axis represent?   Vertical Axis: _____

8. What does the horizontal axis represent?   Horizontal Axis: _____

9. What is the range of values on the scale?   Range: _____ to _____

10. The scale is measured in multiples of _____.   Multiples of _____

Now use the graph to make some comparison statements. Do not look at specific data points. Instead, use the relative lengths of the bars to make these statements.

11. Dawton County has more park and recreation land than

_____

12. Kane County _____

_____

13. _____

_____

Use the information given below to construct a bar graph. Be sure to include a title, labels on both axes, and a source line.

(**Hint:** Make the range of values from 0 to 120. Use multiples of 10.)

The International Atomic Energy Agency stated that in 1998 the United States had 107 nuclear reactors in operation. The agency compared this number to the 59 reactors operating in France, the 29 operating in Russia, and the 16 operating in both Canada and the Ukraine.

14.

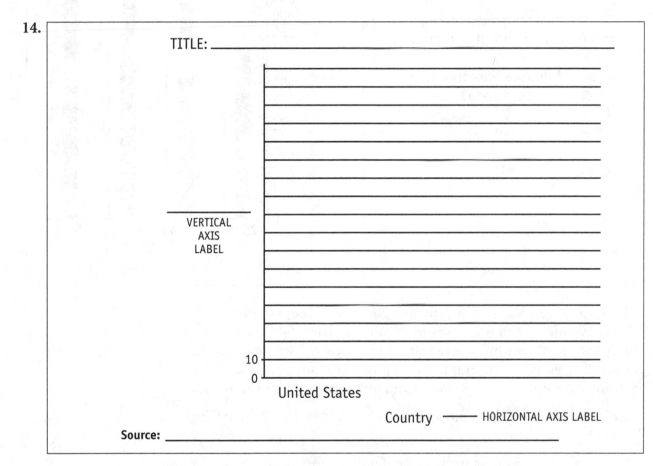

TITLE: _____

VERTICAL AXIS LABEL

10
0

United States

Country ——— HORIZONTAL AXIS LABEL

Source: _____

Now use the graph to make some comparison statements.

15. In 1998 the United States had _____

_____

16. Canada had _____

_____

17. France had _____

_____

Double Bar Graphs

What does the key tell you on this graph?

Why would double bars like these be used to present data?

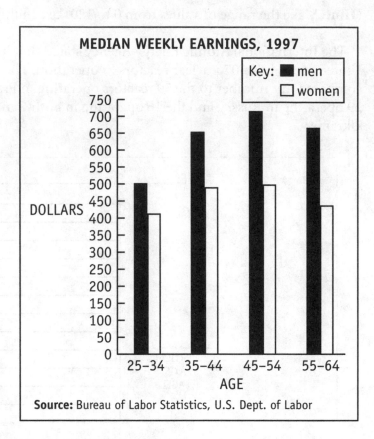

MEDIAN WEEKLY EARNINGS, 1997

Key: ■ men □ women

DOLLARS (y-axis: 0 to 750)

AGE: 25–34, 35–44, 45–54, 55–64

Source: Bureau of Labor Statistics, U.S. Dept. of Labor

This bar graph gives you information about two groups of people—men and women—and uses a **key** to show which bar refers to which group. Instead of creating separate graphs for men and women, a single graph called a **double bar graph** can be used to include both sets of data. You may also have seen graphs with three or more bars side by side.

On a multiple bar graph, more data can be presented without making the graph too hard to read.

For example, if you were interested in finding information about women's median weekly earnings, what type of bar would you look at?

And if you wanted to know what the median weekly earnings were for men age 55–64, where would you look?

Did you answer the **unshaded bars** to the first question and the **last shaded bar** to the second question?

As with all bar graphs, comparisons between groups can easily be made simply by looking at the length of the bars. In double bar graphs, comparisons can be made *within* groups and *between* groups.

EXAMPLE   Using the graph on page 36, you can compare median weekly earnings of men vs. women in the same age group.

You can also compare earnings among different age groups.

....

Write a statement that compares the median weekly earnings of one age group to those of another.

Statement 1: _____

_____

Now write a statement that compares the median weekly earnings of men to those of women.

Statement 2: _____

_____

Here are some sample statements. Do yours sound like these?

- In the United States, men and women age 35–44 earned more than men and women age 25–34.

- In the United States, men of all ages earned more than women.

Use the graph on page 36 to decide if each statement is true or false.

T   F   **1.** The group with the highest median weekly earnings was men age 45–54.

T   F   **2.** At no time between the age of 25 and 64 were women's median weekly earnings higher than the *lowest* weekly earnings for men between the age of 25 and 64.

T   F   **3.** Men's median weekly earnings were at their highest at age 55–64.

T   F   **4.** Women at age 25–34 earned a median weekly earnings of about $430.

Line Graphs

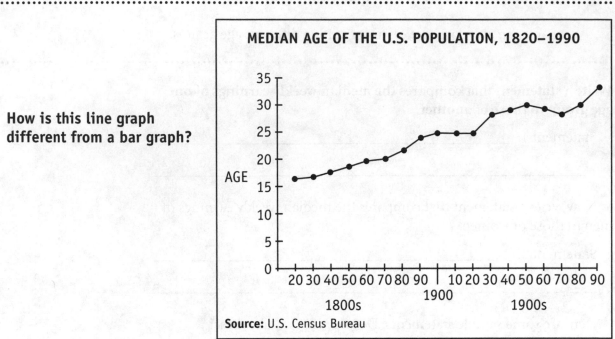

MEDIAN AGE OF THE U.S. POPULATION, 1820–1990

AGE

Source: U.S. Census Bureau

How is this line graph different from a bar graph?

Like a bar graph, a **line graph** uses values plotted along vertical and horizontal axes to display data visually.

You read a line graph in much the same way that you read a bar graph—by finding the point at which the vertical axis value and the horizontal axis value meet, or intersect. Instead of looking at a bar, however, you are looking at a line that may rise or fall, depending on the data.

EXAMPLE What was the median age in the United States in 1920?

STEP 1 Find the year 1920 along the horizontal axis.

STEP 2 Find the point on the line graph directly above 1920.

STEP 3 Move your finger across the graph and find the corresponding value on the vertical axis.

What is the vertical axis value?

ANSWER: The median U.S. age in 1920 was **25 years old.**

A line graph shows values as they change over time. In the line graph on page 38, what value changes over time?

You're right if you said **median age in the United States.** In general, what changes took place between 1820 and 1990? Did the median age go up or down?

Just by looking at the angle of the line, you can see that **the median U.S. age went up,** except in the 1950s and 1960s, when it went down slightly.

Math Recap

Do you know what *median* means? In this case, it means that half the U.S. population is above the age on the graph, and half the population is below. You will learn more about median on page 57.

Use the graph on page 38 to answer the following questions.

1. What was the median U.S. age in 1950?

2. By how much did the median U.S. age go up between 1870 and 1920?

3. A woman is 35 in 1990. Is she above or below the median age in the United States?

Make three statements using the graph on page 38. The first one has been started for you.

4. The median U.S. age was the same in 1980 as it was in

   _____

5. _____

   _____

6. _____

   _____

7. **Critical Thinking**   Based on your knowledge of history, why do you think the median U.S. age went down in the 1950s and 1960s? Were people dying at a younger age? Or was there a greater number of young people for some reason?

More Line Graphs

How is this line graph different from the line graph in the last lesson?

CRUDE OIL PRODUCTION, 1970–1990

BARRELS PRODUCED PER DAY (in millions)

Key:
— United States
----- Saudi Arabia
• • • Mexico

Source: U.S. Department of Energy

As in the line graph on page 38, this graph has years labeled on the horizontal axis, and it shows how certain values change over time. However, this line graph shows *three* separate lines, not just one. Each line represents a separate set of values. The key included on the graph shows what each line refers to.

For example, the solid line (_____) refers to the United States. What do the other two lines refer to?

(• • •) refers to _____.

(– – –) refers to _____.

You're right if you said **Mexico** and **Saudi Arabia,** in that order.

As the title and axes of the graph indicate, all three lines show the changes in crude oil production between 1970 and 1990. Each individual line refers to a particular country.

EXAMPLE   Did the Saudi Arabian crude oil production rise or fall between 1980 and 1985?

STEP 1   Find the line in the key that represents Saudi Arabia.

STEP 2   Find the years 1980 and 1985 on the horizontal axis.

STEP 3   Find the points on the line graph directly above 1980 and 1985.

STEP 4   Move your finger across and find the corresponding values on the vertical axis.

1980 = 10 million
1985 = 3 million

ANSWER: Oil production fell.

Notice that you could also answer the question above without looking at any specific values on the vertical axis. Because the data line is falling between 1980 and 1985, you know that Saudi crude oil production fell during that time.

Use the graph on page 40 to answer the questions.

1. In general, has Mexico's crude oil production risen or fallen between 1970 and 1990?

2. Between 1985 and 1990, did the United States increase or decrease its crude oil production?

3. Which country produced the most crude oil in 1980?

4. Which country produced the most crude oil in 1985?

5. Between 1980 and 1990, which country showed the greatest change in its crude oil production?

6. Use the data from the bar graph below to construct a line graph on a separate sheet of paper.

    STEP 1 Draw and label the vertical and horizontal axes using the same values that are given on the bar graph.

    STEP 2 Read the data for 1995 on the bar graph. On your line graph, put a dot or small × at the same value.

    STEP 3 Continue graphing data for the remaining years.

    STEP 4 When you are finished, connect the data points.

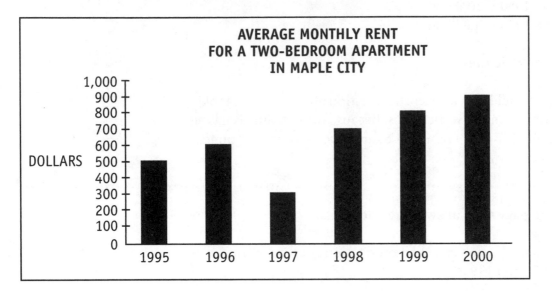

7. Which graph (the bar graph above or the line graph you have just drawn) best shows the change in rental prices?

_____

8. Write a statement comparing the highest average monthly rent with the lowest. _____

_____

_____

9. Write a statement about Maple City rental prices between 1995 and 2000. _____

_____

_____

Visual Statistics

Does this graph look like a line graph?

How is it different from other line graphs you have worked with?

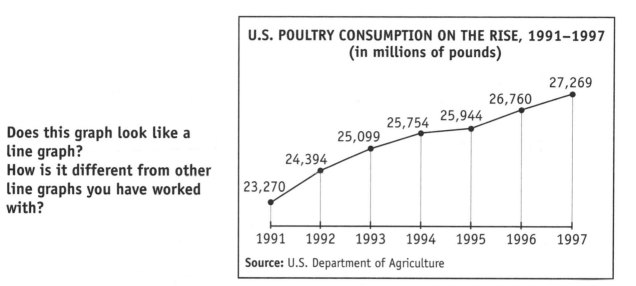

U.S. POULTRY CONSUMPTION ON THE RISE, 1991–1997
(in millions of pounds)

27,269
26,760
25,944
25,754
25,099
24,394
23,270

1991   1992   1993   1994   1995   1996   1997

Source: U.S. Department of Agriculture

Although the graph uses a line to show data points, it is not really a line graph. In this case, no vertical axis is shown.

Some specific points are labeled to show the number of pounds of poultry consumed in 1991, 1992, 1993, 1994, 1995, 1996, and 1997. Instead of finding the exact values on a vertical axis, these points are labeled right on the graph. They're easy to read, aren't they?

Why don't all line graphs label data points like this? Here's why: Suppose you wanted to find the number of pounds of poultry consumed in August 1994. It's not labeled on this graph, and there's no vertical axis with a range of values to provide additional information. On a real line graph, you could estimate the value for August 1994 by using the scale on the vertical axis.

The visual statistics above are terrific if you want to know a general trend about poultry consumption or if you are interested in the specific years labeled. Otherwise, a more complete line graph is better.

Use the visual statistics above to make two statements about poultry consumption in the U.S. The first one has been started for you.

1. Between 1991 and 1997, poultry consumption in the United States

_____

2. _____

_____

Pictographs

Why do you think data is sometimes shown on a pictograph like the one at the right?

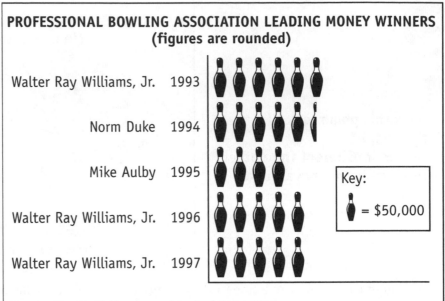

PROFESSIONAL BOWLING ASSOCIATION LEADING MONEY WINNERS
(figures are rounded)

Walter Ray Williams, Jr. 1993

Norm Duke 1994

Mike Aulby 1995

Walter Ray Williams, Jr. 1996

Walter Ray Williams, Jr. 1997

Key:

= $50,000

Source: *The World Almanac and Book of Facts, 1999*

Pictographs are helpful for making comparisons at a glance.

Pictographs are often used in magazines and newspapers because they
- have visual appeal
- are easy to read
- can be easily constructed

This pictograph shows approximations of how much money top bowlers won.

The key tells you that each 🎳 symbol is equal to $50,000.

EXAMPLE   How much money did Mike Aulby win in 1995?

STEP 1   Find the correct year and name on the graph.

STEP 2   Count the number of symbols next to his name.

STEP 3   Multiply 4 by the value given in the key, $50,000.

ANSWER: Mike Aulby won **$200,000** in 1995.

Find and compare other values found in the graph.

1. How much more money did Walter Ray Williams, Jr. earn in 1993 than he did in 1997?

2. Of the years shown, in which year did the leading money winner earn the least amount of money?

3. In what year was Walter Ray Williams, Jr. most recently the leading money winner, and how much did he win?

4. From 1993 to 1997, did all of the leading money winners earn over $150,000?

5. How much money did Norm Duke win in 1994? (**Hint:** Half of the symbol equals $\frac{1}{2}$ of $50,000.)

Use the chart below to construct a pictograph.

- When deciding what dollar value your symbol should represent, look at the largest number you need to graph. Be sure that this amount can be represented in 15 or fewer symbols. More than 15 symbols can become difficult for your reader to count.

- Some suggestions for symbols are circles, squares, Xs, or dollar signs. Or you can create your own symbol.

> **North Invitational Race**
> **Total Prize Money**
>
> 1995: $30,000
> 1996: $40,000
> 1997: $45,000
> 1998: $50,000
> 1999: $60,000
> 2000: $65,000

Write two questions you could ask about the pictograph.

EXAMPLE   Did the prize money stay the same two years in a row?

6. _____

_____

7. _____

_____

Circle Graphs

ORIGIN OF FOREIGN STUDENTS

Latin America and Caribbean
12% Europe
→12%
54% Asia
Middle East 10%
6%
6%
Africa
Other

Source: Institute of International Education

How do you think a circle graph differs from a bar or line graph?

A **circle graph** is a circle divided into parts. The circle represents a *whole,* and each wedge, or section, represents a *part* of that whole.

Add up the percents in the graph above. What total percent is represented by the circle graph?

The circle above represents *all,* or 100%, of the foreign students studying at U.S. colleges. Each part of that whole represents the percent from a specific area of the world.

EXAMPLE   What percent of foreign students studying in the United States are from Africa?

STEP 1   Find the section, or part, labeled *Africa.*

STEP 2   What percent is shown within this section?

ANSWER: 6% of foreign students studying in the United States are from Africa.

Circle graphs are very useful when you want to make comparisons. For example, just by looking at the graph above, you can see that a much larger percent of students come from Asia than from Africa or the Middle East.

Make two statements comparing the percent of students from different regions. The first one has been started for you.

1. There are fewer students from _____

    _____

2. _____

    _____

What does *Other* refer to on the graph? There are often groups of data that are too small to list. These are combined to form one larger section labeled *Other.* In this way, the graph still represents 100% of the data.

"Dollar" Circle Graphs

Circle graphs are usually divided into percents, as is the one on page 46. Sometimes, however, a circle graph is divided into *cents,* or parts of a dollar. Look at the graph at the right.

This graph shows you how many cents out of every dollar went toward various government functions.

For example, out of every dollar collected by the federal government, 25 cents went toward national defense. How many cents went toward grants to states and localities?

You're correct if you said **12¢.**

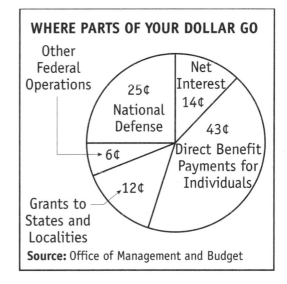

WHERE PARTS OF YOUR DOLLAR GO

Other Federal Operations
Net Interest 14¢
25¢ National Defense
6¢
43¢ Direct Benefit Payments for Individuals
12¢
Grants to States and Localities

Source: Office of Management and Budget

Make a statement comparing the amount of federal money that goes to two different government functions.

3. _____

    _____

Use the information below to label the circle graph. The circle represents a total of 100¢ and the sections are proportional. For example, 43¢ is a little less than $\frac{1}{2}$ of the circle.

4. The United States Office of Management and Budget reports that 34 cents out of every dollar collected by the U.S. government comes from Social Security receipts and 43 cents out of every dollar comes from individual income taxes. Out of each dollar, it is calculated that 11 cents comes from corporation income tax. The remaining 12 cents comes from other sources.

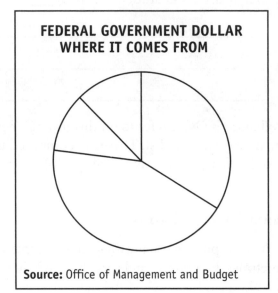

FEDERAL GOVERNMENT DOLLAR WHERE IT COMES FROM

Source: Office of Management and Budget

Make two statements comparing where federal money comes from. The first one has been started for you.

5. More than half of federal money _____

_____

6. _____

_____

Line Plots

1997 Regular NFL Season Final Standings National Conference	
Team	**Number of Wins**
New York Giants	10
Philadelphia Eagles	6
Washington Redskins	8
Arizona Cardinals	4
Dallas Cowboys	6
Minnesota Vikings	9
Green Bay Packers	13
Detroit Lions	9
Chicago Bears	4
Tampa Bay Buccaneers	10
San Francisco 49ers	13
Los Angeles Rams	5
New Orleans Saints	6
Atlanta Falcons	7

What was the most common number of wins by teams in the National Football Conference in 1997?

A **line plot** is often used to show data in a more visual way than the chart above. Construct a line plot and see what advantages it has.

STEP 1 Draw a line across your paper.

STEP 2 Find the scale you are working with. (In this case, the fewest number of wins is 4, and the greatest is 13.) Write these numbers under your line as shown and fill in the values in between.

STEP 3 Now use an × to record each number of wins on the number line. (The Giants had 10 wins, so put an × above the 10 on the number line.)

STEP 4 Continue marking the ×s in a stack above the appropriate numbers. (The values for the Eagles, the Redskins, the Cardinals, the Cowboys, and the Vikings are now added.)

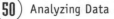

What types of things can you see more clearly from a line plot than you can from a chart of data?

You may have seen a couple of things just "jump out at you" that perhaps were not as obvious when you read the chart.

- There is a **cluster** of ×s around a certain area of the line. Where is this bunch, or group, of ×s? You're right if you said **between 5 and 7**. This cluster of ×s tells you that 5, 6, or 7 wins was a more common occurrence than, say, 11 or 12 wins.

- There are single data points on the line that are quite a bit above or below the cluster. From these, it is also easy to see the highest and lowest values in the data collected.

Line plots make it easy to compare individual values at a glance. For instance, do teams generally win about 10 games, or more than that?

· ·

Use the data below to create your own line plot.
- **Read the number of representatives for each state and put an ×**
  above that value on the line plot.
- **The first five states on the list have been marked for you.**

1. **Number of Members in the House of Representatives, by State, 1998**

✓	Alabama	7	Louisiana	7	Ohio	19
✓	Alaska	2	Maine	2	Oklahoma	6
✓	Arizona	6	Maryland	8	Oregon	5
✓	Arkansas	4	Massachusetts	10	Pennsylvania	21
✓	California	52	Michigan	16	Rhode Island	2
	Colorado	6	Minnesota	8	South Carolina	6
	Connecticut	6	Mississippi	5	South Dakota	2
	Delaware	2	Missouri	9	Tennessee	9
	Florida	23	Montana	2	Texas	30
	Georgia	11	Nebraska	3	Utah	3
	Hawaii	2	Nevada	2	Vermont	2
	Idaho	2	New Hampshire	2	Virginia	11
	Illinois	20	New Jersey	13	Washington	9
	Indiana	10	New Mexico	3	West Virginia	3
	Iowa	5	New York	31	Wisconsin	9
	Kansas	4	North Carolina	12	Wyoming	2
	Kentucky	6	North Dakota	2		

2. What is the least number of representatives from a state, and how many states have that many?

3. What is the greatest number of representatives? Are there many states that have close to this number of representatives?

4. Is there a cluster of values in a certain area of the line plot? Where is it?

5. Representation in the House is based on state population. The larger the state population, the greater the number of representatives. Make two statements about population based on the information above. The first one has been started for you.

   a. Many states have _____

   _____

   b. _____

   _____

6. **Critical Thinking** Each state in the United States is represented by two members in the Senate, regardless of the state's population. Why do you think membership in the House of Representatives is based on population? Is it fair that states with more people have more representatives?

Scatter Diagrams

An employee of a cereal manufacturer said to his boss, "I have this theory that the more sugar we put in our breakfast cereals, the more kids will like them. What do you think?" "Brilliant!" replied the boss. "Let's collect some data and check it out." Here's the data they came up with:

Cereal	Teaspoons of Sugar per Serving	Number of Children Who Liked It
Good for You	1	2
Sweeties	8	19
YumYums	4	12
SugarPlus	5	11
PlainPuffs	2	5
Sugar City	9	20
Kiddo Krunch	5	13
Sweethearts	8	17
Munchies	6	12

Is the employee's theory correct?
Can you tell by looking at the chart?

You may have noticed that it is difficult to prove the employee's theory by simply looking at the data. An excellent way to display this type of data is with a **scatter diagram.** The diagram below shows the intersection of amount of sugar and number of children.

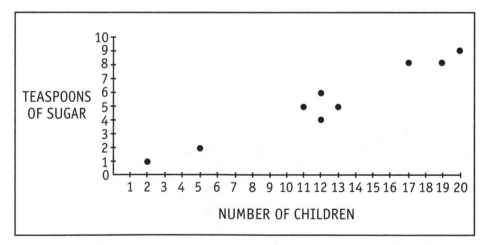

Can you tell from this diagram whether the cereal company employee's theory is true? Does more sugar mean that more kids like the cereal?

The answer is **yes.** As the number of teaspoons of sugar goes up, so does the number of kids who like the cereal. In general, as one number gets larger, the other number gets larger. This means that there is a **correlation,** or a relationship between the two values.

A research group did an informal study of the relationship between people's income and the number of years of school they had completed.

Some responses have already been plotted on the scatter diagram below.

Respondent	Years of School	Income
2E	16	$30,000
2F	10	28,000
2G	14	21,000
3A	14	20,000
3B	8	7,000
3C	9	10,000
3D	9	11,000
3E	15	30,000
3F	16	25,000
3G	16	12,000

Now plot the responses listed in the chart at the right. For each respondent, put a point at the intersection of the two values: years of school and income.

1.

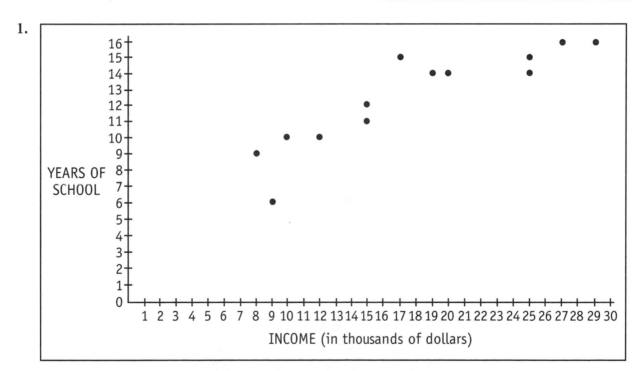

2. In general, do you see a correlation between number of school years and income? Write a statement about the data based on your scatter diagram.

_____

_____

Arithmetic Mean

"You are getting a fantastic deal on this apartment," says a landlord. "This beautiful place for only $400 per month! The average rental rate for two-bedroom apartments in this neighborhood is almost $500. If you want to live in this area, you can't do better than this place."

Sounds like a good deal, doesn't it?
Assuming that the landlord did the math correctly, could you get a two-bedroom apartment for much less than $400?

What Is a Typical Value?

You have seen how data and statistics can be represented on graphs, charts, and diagrams. Another way that statistics are often presented is in the form of **typical values.**

For example, you might say that the *most common* age of a high school senior is 17 years old. This does not mean that *all* high school seniors are 17, but that many are 17 and most are *close* to 17.

There are three different ways to describe a typical value: finding the **mean,** the **median,** and the **mode.** In fact, the landlord above is not really giving the renter enough information to make a decision about rental prices in the area. Let's see why.

Arithmetic mean, or just **mean,** is another way of saying **average.**

Follow these steps to find the mean of a set of data.

STEP 1   Add up the numbers.

STEP 2   Divide the sum by the number of numbers in your set of data.

Here are the rental rates in the neighborhood.

1200 Speen St.	$250	1320 Day St.	$240
1202 Speen St.	250	1322 Day St.	220
1203 Speen St.	240	1400 Day St.	250
1211 Speen St.	250	1401 Day St.	250
1220 Speen St.	250	400 North Ave.	250
320 Ashland Ave.	270	402 North Ave.	290
330 Ashland Ave.	240	404 North Ave.	270
333 Ashland Ave.	260	406 North Ave.	260
440 Ashland Ave.	230	408 North Ave.	1,700
500 Ashland Ave.	250	410 North Ave.	1,650
1111 Day St.	290	412 North Ave.	1,600
1290 Day St.	250	414 North Ave.	1,700

<u>EXAMPLE</u>   What is the mean of the rental rates listed?

> **STEP 1** Add up the numbers in the set of data.
>
> The total is $11,710.
>
> **STEP 2** Count the number of rental rates listed.
>
> There are 24 numbers in this set of data.
>
> **STEP 3** Divide the sum by the number of numbers in the set of data.
>
> $11,710 ÷ 24 = $487.92

ANSWER: The mean is $487.92.

As the landlord stated, the average (mean) of rental rates is "almost $500." However, look again at the rates listed. Are any of the values even close to $500? No. In fact, most of the values *center around $250.*

The mean is so high because of the four very high rental rates of $1,700, $1,600, $1,700, and $1,650. These rates are so much higher than the others that they raise the mean to an amount that is not really typical!

Is the landlord on page 54 not telling the truth? Is it possible to tell the truth but still be misleading?

....

Find the mean (average) in each set of data below.

1. Distance from home to workplace among employees: 2.8 miles, 4.8 miles, 8 miles, 1.5 miles, 3 miles, 6 miles, 2.5 miles, 3.4 miles

2. Weekly grocery bills: $90, $120, $48, $55, $37

3. Tips earned: $35, $48, $22, $18, $25, $32, $44

Median

Look at a second way to describe the rental rate data on page 54.

The **median** of a set of data is the middle value when the pieces of data are ordered from least to greatest value.

EXAMPLE 1 What is the median in this data set?

56	61	49	32	90	75	23	101	70

STEP 1 Put the set of data in order, from least to greatest value.

23	32	49	56	61	70	75	90	101

STEP 2 Select the value in the middle of the set.

23	32	49	56	(61)	70	75	90	101

ANSWER: The median value in this set of data is 61.

However, when there is an even number of values in a set of data, the median is the *mean* of the middle two numbers.

EXAMPLE 2 What is the median in this data set?

20, 21, (22, 23) 24, 25

STEP 1 Add the two middle numbers.

$$22 + 23 = 45$$

STEP 2 Divide by 2.

$$45 \div 2 = 22\frac{1}{2}$$

ANSWER: $22\frac{1}{2}$ is the median of the set.

Looking back to the rental rates given on page 54, the *median* rental rate is $250.

Can you see that the *median* value of $250 is much more representative of the rental rates in this neighborhood than the mean value of $487?

Find the median in each set of data below.

1. Calculator prices among area stores: $9.50, $12.00, $14.50, $12.00, $12.50, $13.00

2. Height of South High basketball players: 6′2″, 6′10″, 7′3″, 7′4″, 5′11″

Mode

Now look at the third way to find a typical value. The **mode** in a set of data is the number that occurs most frequently in the set.

EXAMPLE   What is the mode in this set of data?

| 21 | 15 | 70 | 22 | 21 | 71 | 21 | 15 | 40 |

How many times does each number appear?

21: 3   70: 1   71: 1

15: 2   22: 1   40: 1

ANSWER: The mode is 21, since it appears most often in the set of data.

What is the mode of the rental rates given on page 54?

1. Determine how many times each value appears in the set of data. (This process has been started for you.)

    1,700: __2__   260: _____

    1,650: _____   250: _____

    1,600: _____   240: _____

    290: _____   230: _____

    270: _____   220: _____

2. The value that appears most frequently is the mode. What is the mode?

Again, in this case, the **mode** gives you a better picture of the rental rates in the area than the mean does.

(**Note:** Sometimes there is no mode in a set of data because each value appears only once. In this case, use mean or median to express the typical value.)

Find the mode in each set of data below.

3. Prices of a 1-pound box of salt in area stores: $0.57, $0.49, $0.52, $0.49, $0.57, $0.49

4. Number of weeks on Top 40 radio: 8, 10, 5, 3, 9, 10, 10, 9, 5, 8, 4, 2

Mean, Median, and Mode

Is mode or median always a better way to show the typical value than the mean? No. In the case of the landlord on page 54, it certainly would have been fairer to the potential renter to use median or mode. However, there are other cases where the mean *does* give a more accurate picture of the typical value.

> Use the mean to show typical value *unless* there are extreme values in the set of data. Extreme values are those that are not typical of the rest of the data.

For each set of data below, find the mean, the median, and the mode. Then decide which method best represents the most typical value in each set.

1. **Dollars Collected by Charity Groups**

Cancer Fund	$1,100
Grand Foundation	300
Women for Women	1,100
John Kramer Fund	650
Heart & Lung Assn.	500
Dalmore Committee	230

   Mean: _____

   Median: _____

   Mode: _____

   Best representation of typical value: _____

2. **Attendance at Plainville Pirates Baseball Games**

June 15 game	230 people
June 16 game	175 people
June 30 game	225 people
July 4 game	700 people
July 5 game	225 people
July 12 game	185 people
July 14 game	200 people
July 20 game	180 people
July 27 game	165 people

   Mean: _____

   Median: _____

   Mode: _____

   Best representation of typical value: _____

Critical Thinking with Data

Suppose a local school system is deciding how much money to allot to its high school sports program. Part of its decision is based on how much the surrounding school systems spend on their programs.

Use the graph below and your knowledge of typical values to answer the questions that follow.

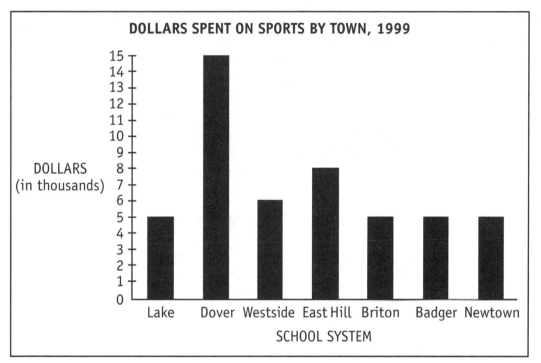

1. Suppose you are a high school football coach in the Westside school system. You want your school system to spend as much money as possible on the sports program. Would you use mean, median, or mode to show that Westside spends too little? Write a paragraph persuading the school system to spend more money. Use any data you need from the graph above.

2. Now imagine that you are a Westside school department member, and you are tired of having so much money spent on sports. You would rather have more money allotted for teachers' salaries. Would you use mean, median, or mode to show that Westside spends too much on sports? Write a paragraph defending your point of view. Use any data you need from the graph above.

Group Project: Organizing Data

Remember all those questionnaires you filled out back in the last chapter? Now it's time to make some sense of all that information. If you are working in a group, add the numbers you came up with on page 27 to the numbers obtained by the rest of your group.

Chart/Table

STEP 1   Divide your questionnaires into Male and Female groups.

STEP 2   Divide each of these two groups into a Day Person group and a Night Owl group. (You should have four groups.) Count up each group and record the numbers below.

STEP 3   Put all questionnaires back into Male/Female groupings.

STEP 4   Divide them once again, this time into a Lives Alone group and a Lives with Others group. (You should have four new groups.) Count up each group and record the numbers below.

STEP 5   Make a statement about the data you have organized.

	Male	Female
Day Person		
Night Owl		
Lives Alone		
Lives with Others		

Statement: _____

_____

_____

Line Plot

From page 27, use the information you collected in answer to "How many hours of television do you watch per week?" to complete the line plot below. Make a statement about the data you have plotted.

Hours of Television per Week

Statement: _____

_____

Scatter Diagram

STEP 1 From page 27, use the data from these questions:

"How many times per week do you see people for a social occasion?"

"How many close friends do you have, not including family?"

STEP 2 Label one axis below "Number of Social Occasions" and the other "Number of Close Friends."

STEP 3 Label the scale for each axis. Be sure to take into account the range of values for each set of data.

STEP 4 Plot the data.

STEP 5 Make a statement about the data you have plotted.

Statement: _____

_____

ANALYZING DATA

The Purpose of a Graph or Chart

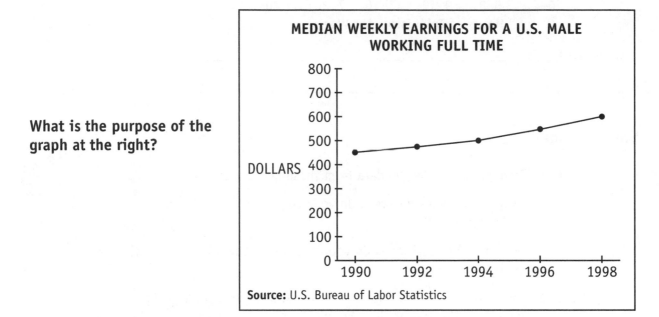

MEDIAN WEEKLY EARNINGS FOR A U.S. MALE WORKING FULL TIME

Source: U.S. Bureau of Labor Statistics

What is the purpose of the graph at the right?

Your first step in analyzing data is to understand the *topic* of the data. Many times, mistakes are made in interpreting data because a reader did not understand the goal, or purpose, of a graph or chart. For example, circle the letter of the statement that accurately summarizes the purpose of the graph.

For the period 1990 to 1998, the graph shows the rise in

  a. median weekly earnings in the United States

  b. median weekly earnings for a U.S. male working full-time

  c. median weekly earnings for a U.S. male

You're correct if you chose statement **b.** What's wrong with the other two?

1. If the first statement were true, you could expect to find information about *female* workers. The graph title clearly states *male* workers.

2. If the third statement were true, you could expect to find information about *part-time* workers' earning. The graph title specifies *full time*.

Only statement **b** accurately summarizes the graph's purpose.

To understand the purpose of a chart, graph, or table, you need to use information from the *title* and *labels*. Ask yourself these basic questions:

- *What* data is being presented?

- *When*, or over what period of time, does the data apply?

- *Where*, or what location, is the data concerned with?

- *How* is the data presented (in dollars? in miles per hour? in average cost?)

....

Fill in the blanks to summarize the purpose of the chart below.

The chart shows the

_____
what?

in _____
where?

in _____
when?

in _____
how?

(among fields employing at least 5,000 people).

Highest-Paying Jobs* in N. Essex County, 1999	
Profession	**Average Weekly Salary**
Lawyer	$990
Airline Pilot	807
Chemical Engineer	807
Electrical Engineer	803
Aerospace Engineer	801
Physician	792
Mechanical Engineer	766

*Among fields employing at least 5,000 people

An accurate summary of the purpose for the chart above is:

The chart shows the _____ *highest-paying job* _____
what?

in _____ *the N. Essex County* _____
where?

in ____ *1999* ____ in ____ *average weekly salary* ____
when?   how?

(among fields employing at least 5,000 people).

Of course, there are other ways to summarize a graph or chart. Using your own words, state the purpose of the graph. Be sure to include the *what, when, where,* and *how* information in some form.

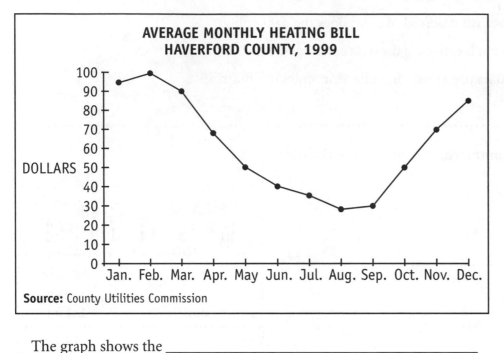

**AVERAGE MONTHLY HEATING BILL
HAVERFORD COUNTY, 1999**

Source: County Utilities Commission

The graph shows the _____
what?

in _____ in _____
where?   when?

in _____.
how?

Does your summary sound something like this?
The graph shows the average monthly heating bill in Haverford County in 1999 in dollars.

The Source of Data

All good graphs, charts, and tables name the **source** that collected and organized the data. A **source line** is usually printed somewhere beneath the data.

The source of any data is important to know in case you have questions about the data or its reliability.

What is the source of the data for the graph above?

_____

Decide if the summary given for each set of data below is accurate. If it is not, which information is inaccurate—the *what, where, when,* or *how?*

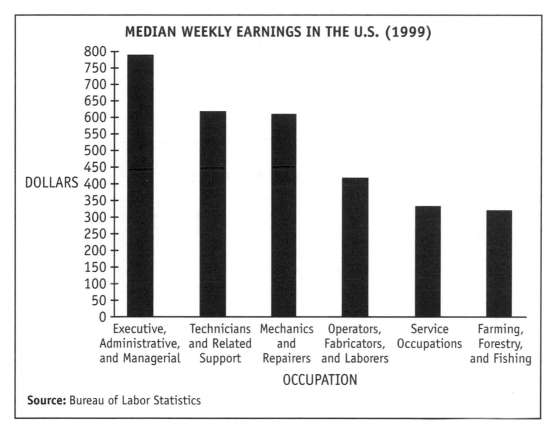

MEDIAN WEEKLY EARNINGS IN THE U.S. (1999)

DOLLARS

OCCUPATION

Executive, Administrative, and Managerial | Technicians and Related Support | Mechanics and Repairers | Operators, Fabricators, and Laborers | Service Occupations | Farming, Forestry, and Fishing

Source: Bureau of Labor Statistics

1. The purpose of the graph above is to show the 1999 median weekly earnings for the best-paying jobs in the United States, in dollars.

   Is the summary accurate?

   If not, explain why.

2. The purpose of the graph at the right is to show the price of milk from 1997 to 2001 in dollars per quart.

   Is the summary accurate?

   If not, explain why.

MILK PRICES AT CRESENT FARM DAIRY

DOLLARS PER QUART

1997   1998   1999   2000   2001*

Source: County Dairy Association

* projected

Americans Believe It's All Right to Lie

	% Men	% Women
to protect oneself	63	52
to avoid personal embarrassment	56	48
to keep one's job	56	35
to gain a small amount of money	25	15

Source: *Press Mentor* survey

3. The purpose of the chart above is to show how many Americans lie at certain times.

   Is the summary accurate?

   If not, explain why.

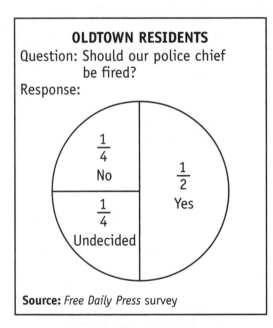

OLDTOWN RESIDENTS

Question: Should our police chief be fired?

Response:

$\frac{1}{4}$ No

$\frac{1}{2}$ Yes

$\frac{1}{4}$ Undecided

Source: *Free Daily Press* survey

4. The purpose of the graph above is to show what fraction of Oldtown residents were in favor of, not in favor of, or undecided about firing the police chief.

   Is the summary accurate?

   If not, explain why.

Reading Data: Be Specific

The vertical axis value of the data point circled is between 25 and 30. The horizontal axis value is between '65 and '95.

But does the graph tell you more about the circled data point?

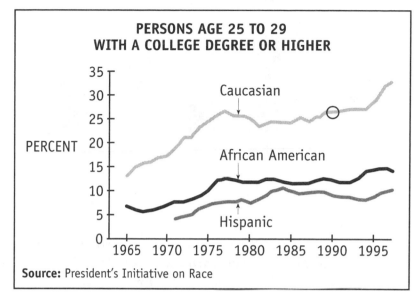

PERSONS AGE 25 TO 29 WITH A COLLEGE DEGREE OR HIGHER

Source: President's Initiative on Race

In order to be as accurate as possible when making statements about specific data points, you need to use *all* of the information provided, including labels on *both* axes.

Look at the circled data point on the graph. Circle the *most accurate* and *specific* statement about that data point.

- In 1990, 26 Caucasian people age 25 to 29 had a college degree or higher.

- Between 1965 and 1995, 26% of Caucasian people age 25 to 29 had a college degree or higher.

- In 1990, 26% of Caucasian people age 25 to 29 had a college degree or higher.

Now look at each statement in detail.

1. *In 1990, 26 Caucasian people age 25 to 29 had a college degree or higher.*   False

   This statement does not take into account the label on the vertical axis—*Percent.* Twenty-six *percent* of Caucasian people age 25 to 29 had a college degree or higher.

2. *Between 1965 and 1995, 26% of Caucasian people age 25 to 29 had a college degree or higher.*   Not Specific

   Not all of the years showed this 26% figure. You can figure out the specific year shown by looking at the horizontal axis. The year at the circled data point is 1990.

3. *In 1990, 26% of Caucasian people age 25 to 29 had a college degree or higher.*   Accurate

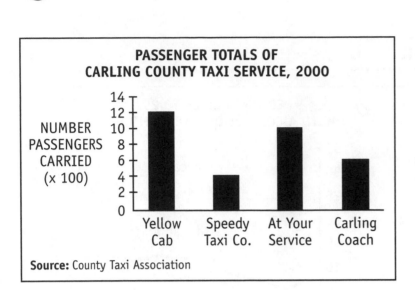

**PASSENGER TOTALS OF
CARLING COUNTY TAXI SERVICE, 2000**

NUMBER
PASSENGERS
CARRIED
(x 100)

Yellow Cab | Speedy Taxi Co. | At Your Service | Carling Coach

Source: County Taxi Association

Tell why each of the following is *not* a precise statement about the data in the graph above. In other words, what additional information could be given to make each statement true or more accurate?

EXAMPLE   In 2000, the Yellow Cab company carried 800 times as many passengers as Speedy Taxi Co. did.

The Yellow Cab company carried 800 more

passengers, not 800 times as many.

1. In 2000, the Yellow Cab company in Carling County carried 12 passengers.

   _____

   _____

2. At Your Service carried 1,000 passengers.

   _____

   _____

3. The Carling Coach bar goes up to 600 on the graph.

   _____

   _____

Using the graph on page 68, choose four phrases from the list below to make four different statements about the data. Be sure to use
- **information from the title of the graph**
- **information from *both* axes**
- **labels**

Phrases

$\frac{1}{3}$ the number of passengers	more passengers than
twice as many	800 more passengers than
half as many	200 fewer passengers than
the greatest number of	the fewest

EXAMPLE   In 2000, Speedy Taxi Co. carried the fewest passengers among the four taxi services listed.

4. _____

_____

5. _____

_____

6. _____

_____

7. _____

_____

Reading Data: Using Only the Information Given

In the United States, what state had the greatest number of hazardous waste sites in 1998? Can you tell from this graph?

HAZARDOUS WASTE SITES IN SELECTED STATES, 1998
(general superfund sites)

Key:
= 10 Sites

Source: U.S. Environmental Protection Agency

You might be tempted to answer New Jersey to the question above. Of the states *listed on this graph,* New Jersey does, in fact, have the greatest number. However, look closely at the title of the graph. Notice that only *selected* states are shown. A state that is not shown might have a greater number of hazardous waste sites than New Jersey. *The graph simply does not give us that information.*

In this lesson, you will work on using *only* the information on the graph.

Make a statement about Wisconsin's hazardous waste sites using the data from the graph. Remember to include only information from
- **the title**
- **the data given**
- **the key**

Statement: _____

_____

_____

Does your statement sound something like this?

Wisconsin has about 40 hazardous waste sites.

The following statements about the graph *are not accurate.* Put a check mark next to the information listed below each statement that is *not* supported by the graph and therefore *cannot* support such a statement.

1. According to the U.S. Environmental Protection Agency, Florida residents were more willing to store hazardous waste than the citizens of Virginia.

    _____ **a.** There are more hazardous waste sites in Florida than in Virginia.

    _____ **b.** Florida residents are willing to store hazardous waste.

    _____ **c.** Virginia residents fought hard against hazardous waste sites.

2. Maryland, with 10 hazardous waste sites, is a more dangerous place to live than West Virginia with only four sites.

    _____ **a.** The sites in Maryland are better contained than those in West Virginia.

    _____ **b.** Maryland has more sites than West Virginia.

    _____ **c.** Maryland also has more crime than West Virginia.

3. West Virginia has the fewest hazardous waste sites in the United States.

    _____ **a.** West Virginia has four hazardous waste sites.

    _____ **b.** Hazardous waste sites are listed for all 50 states.

   You should have checked the following information that cannot be supported by the graph.

1. **b., c.** From the given information, you have no way of knowing how residents reacted.

2. **a., c.** No information is provided about the condition of the sites or the crime rate for any of the states.

3. **b.** Hazardous waste sites are listed for only eight states.

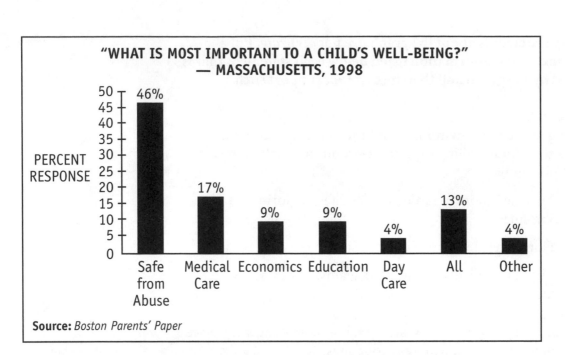

"WHAT IS MOST IMPORTANT TO A CHILD'S WELL-BEING?" — MASSACHUSETTS, 1998

PERCENT RESPONSE

Safe from Abuse: 46%
Medical Care: 17%
Economics: 9%
Education: 9%
Day Care: 4%
All: 13%
Other: 4%

Source: *Boston Parents' Paper*

State why each of the following is *not* an accurate statement about the data in the graph above.

EXAMPLE   Nine percent of people responding to a Massachusetts poll felt that their children's education was unsatisfactory.

The graph refers to how people answered the question, "What is most important to a child's well-being?" Respondents were not necessarily dissatisfied.

1. During the year 1998, just under half of all Massachusetts children were victims of abuse.

   _____

   _____

2. Forty-six people responded that safety from abuse was the most important factor to a child's well-being.

   _____

   _____

3. More Americans believe that medical care is more important to a child's well-being than quality of day care services.

   _____

   _____

The Language of Estimation

What did a barrel of crude oil cost in 1983?
Is it easy to determine from this graph? Why?

WORLD CRUDE OIL PRICES

PER BARREL COST (in 1997 dollars)

$63.51

$4.30

$12.01

1970   1979   1998

Source: Cambridge Energy Research Assoc.

Many graphs are not meant to display exact figures. For example, on the graph above, it is impossible to tell the *exact* price of a barrel of oil in any year except those labeled—1970, 1979, and 1998. All you can really see is that the data point for 1983, for example, is somewhere between $30 and $40.

This doesn't mean that the graph is poorly constructed. Different graphs have different purposes. If you want to find a value on a graph like the one above, you'll need to **estimate**.

There are many ways to express estimates. Use your knowledge of the words in italic to decide if each statement is true or false according to the graph above. Circle T or F.

T F   **1.** The price of a barrel of crude oil in 1995 was *more than* $15.

T F   **2.** The price of a barrel of crude oil in 1980 was *less than* $60.

T F   **3.** The *approximate* price of a barrel of crude oil in 1990 was $30.

You are correct if you found that the first two statements are true. The 1995 data point is somewhere around $20. In 1980 the price fell below the $60 line.

Did you find that the third statement is false? The data point is clearly below the $30 line. Therefore, it is more accurate to say that the approximate price in 1990 was $20.

There are many ways in which estimates can be expressed. Look at the following list of words and phrases taken from a newspaper. All of them tell the reader that the number given is an estimate.

- *almost* a quarter of a million dollars

- the lot measured *just over* 13 acres

- totaling *about* a thousand

- *less than* the average of $14,500

- needing *close to* 7 hours to complete

Use the graph to fill in the blanks below. Choose your answers from the list given.

Choose from this list:

    less than
    more than
    almost
    approximately
    estimated to be
    between

(**Note:** More than one choice may be correct.)

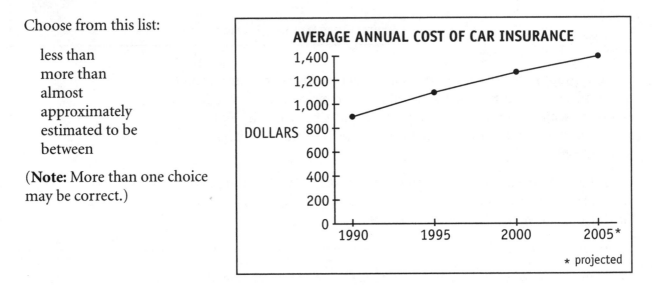

AVERAGE ANNUAL COST OF CAR INSURANCE

* projected

1. In 1995 the average annual cost of car insurance was
   _____ $1,000.

2. The average annual cost of car insurance was _____
   $800 and $1,000 in 1990.

3. The difference in annual car insurance between 2000 and 2005 is
   expected to be _____ $100.

Make two statements using estimates of the data on the graph.

4. _____

   _____

5. _____

   _____

Accurate Estimating

Read the two newspaper articles below. Do they contradict each other?

The Daily Journal
. . . in fact, in the year 2001, there will be 11 million women between the ages of 40 and 44 in the U.S., and approximately the same number of men in that age group . . .

Daily Express
. . . the projection for the number of men between 40 and 44 in the U.S. in the year 2001 is about 11,400,000—slightly more than the number of women in that age group . . .

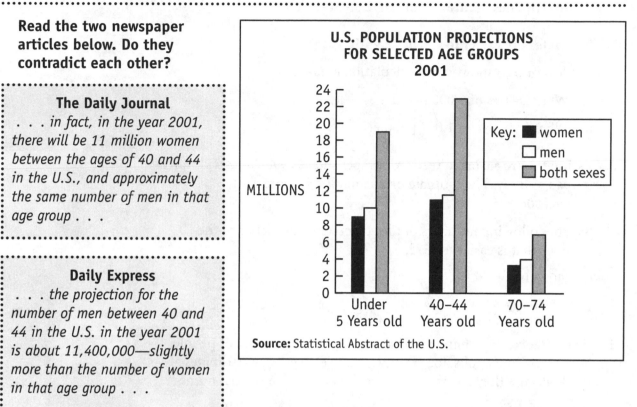

U.S. POPULATION PROJECTIONS FOR SELECTED AGE GROUPS 2001

MILLLIONS

Key: ■ women □ men ▨ both sexes

Under 5 Years old · 40–44 Years old · 70–74 Years old

Source: Statistical Abstract of the U.S.

Which newspaper is reporting the correct figures? Will there be 11 million men age 40–44 in the U.S. in 2001, or more?

Remember, *estimates are not exact.* The fact is that *both* newspaper articles above give acceptable estimates of the data. With estimates, 11.4 million can be considered about 11 million.

Estimate an answer to the problem at the right. Do *not* find an exact number.

$$3{,}675 + 199 \approx$$

Which did you find as your estimate: 3,875; 3,900; or 4,000?

Whichever estimate you found, you are correct. In fact, any figure close to one of those above is a good estimate!

Depending on how close to the actual answer you need to be, an estimate can have a wide range of values.

Why Estimate?

Why are estimates used so often? Here are some reasons.

1. **Estimates are easier to calculate with.**

   Circle **a** or **b** to show which calculation is easier.

   a. What is 40% of 1,000 people?

   b. What is 39.8% of 1,019 people?

2. **Estimates are easier to read.** A number such as 998,786 is awkward to read and say. The estimate of one million is more easily understood.

   Say the following numbers out loud and circle the letter of the number that is easier to read.

   a. 2,000,000

   b. 2,001,112

3. **Exact figures can change frequently.** The exact number of people living in Minneapolis, for example, changes every day. Estimates are used because they are as close as we can come to the actual number.

   Which of the following questions needs only an estimate for an answer?

   a. How many people are employed in the auto industry?

   b. How many passengers can the new Ford van carry?

4. **Exact figures are often not necessary.**

   As a consumer, which of the following would you want an exact figure for?

   a. the total cost of a microwave oven you want to buy

   b. the number of microwave ovens a store has in stock

Did you circle **a** for each question above? If so, you are understanding the purpose of estimation!

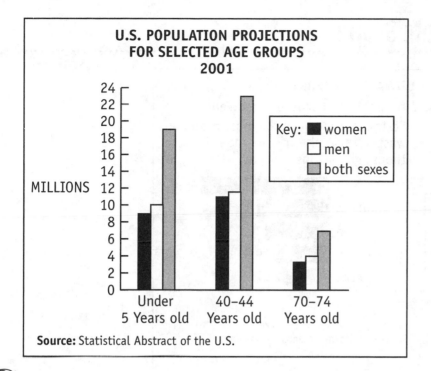

U.S. POPULATION PROJECTIONS FOR SELECTED AGE GROUPS 2001

Key: ■ women □ men ▨ both sexes

Source: Statistical Abstract of the U.S.

Use the data to fill in the blanks that follow. Be sure to use words such as *about* or *approximately* when appropriate.

1. In 2001 there will be _____ 7 million people between the ages of 70 and 74.

2. In 2001 there will be about _____ times as many women 40–44 years old than women 70–74 years old.

3. Of the 19 million children under 5 years old in 2001, _____ will be boys.

4. In 2001 there will be more than _____ times as many children under age 5 than men 70–74 years old.

Look in a newspaper or magazine and find two places in which an estimate is used instead of an exact number.

5. How do you know an estimate is being used?

_____

_____

6. Why do you think an estimate is used instead of an exact number?

_____

_____

Using More than One Data Source

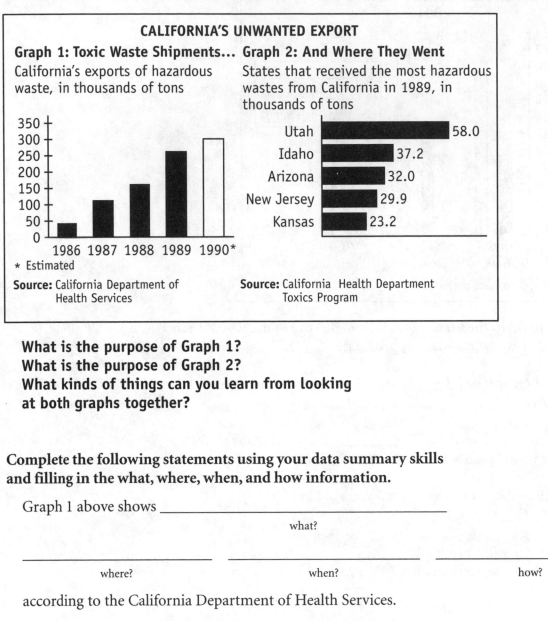

CALIFORNIA'S UNWANTED EXPORT

Graph 1: Toxic Waste Shipments...
California's exports of hazardous waste, in thousands of tons

Graph 2: And Where They Went
States that received the most hazardous wastes from California in 1989, in thousands of tons

Utah 58.0
Idaho 37.2
Arizona 32.0
New Jersey 29.9
Kansas 23.2

* Estimated

Source: California Department of Health Services

Source: California Health Department Toxics Program

What is the purpose of Graph 1?
What is the purpose of Graph 2?
What kinds of things can you learn from looking at both graphs together?

Complete the following statements using your data summary skills and filling in the what, where, when, and how information.

Graph 1 above shows _____
                              what?

_____   _____   _____
        where?   when?   how?

according to the California Department of Health Services.

Graph 2 shows _____
                        what?

_____   _____   _____
        where?   when?   how?

according to the California Health Department Toxics Program.

Your summaries should sound something like this:

Graph 1 shows **toxic waste shipments in California in 1986 through 1990 in thousands of tons,** according to the California Department of Health Services.

Graph 2 shows **the five states that received the most hazardous waste from California in 1989, in thousands of tons,** according to the California Health Department Toxics Program.

What information can you get by using *both* graphs that you can't get by using just one of them?

For example, the following question can be answered only if you use *both* graphs.

EXAMPLE   What *percent* of California's toxic waste exports was received by Utah in 1989?

STEP 1   Graph 1 tells you that California exported 250,000 tons of toxic waste in 1989.

STEP 2   Graph 2 tells you that 58,000 tons went to Utah.

STEP 3   What percent of 250,000 is 58,000?

$58,000 \div 250,000 = 0.232 = 23.2\%$

ANSWER: Utah received 23.2% of California's toxic waste in 1989.

....

Which of the graphs on page 78 do you need to answer these questions? Circle Graph 1, Graph 2, or Both. If the question cannot be answered by either of the graphs, circle Neither.

1. How many tons of hazardous waste did   Graph 1   Graph 2   Both   Neither
    California export to Kansas in 1989?

2. What fraction of California's toxic waste   Graph 1   Graph 2   Both   Neither
    exports went to New Jersey in 1989?

3. How many tons of toxic waste existed in   Graph 1   Graph 2   Both   Neither
    Arizona in 1989?

4. How many tons of toxic waste are estimated   Graph 1   Graph 2   Both   Neither
    to be exported from California in 1990?

MILLTOWN HIGH SCHOOL 1999 AGE BREAKDOWN
Total Student Population: 1,400

Source: Milltown School Committee

STUDENTS PARTICIPATING IN SCHOOL ACTIVITIES	
Activity	Number of Participants
Student government	210
Music/Band	140
Intramural sports	425
Library club	80
Social committee	120

For part a of each question, decide whether you need to use the graph, the chart, or both to answer the question. If the question cannot be answered using any of the information above, circle Neither.

For part b, answer the question if possible.

5. What fraction of the Milltown student population participated in music/band activities in 1999?

   a. Graph   Chart   Both   Neither

   b. Answer:

6. Assuming that participation in all activities is not affected by age, how many 16-year-olds were in the Library Club?

   a. Graph   Chart   Both   Neither

   b. Answer:

7. How many 13-year-olds attended Milltown High?

   a. Graph   Chart   Both   Neither

   b. Answer:

8. How many girls played intramural sports at Milltown High?

   a. Graph   Chart   Both   Neither

   b. Answer:

Putting Data in Different Forms

What percent of Johnson Public Housing residents were registered to vote in 1998? Can you answer this question based on the information given?

REGISTERED VOTERS IN JOHNSON PUBLIC HOUSING COMPLEX

TOTAL RESIDENTS IN JOHNSON PUBLIC HOUSING

1996	3,900
1997	3,450
1998	3,500
1999	3,280
2000	2,500

Source: League of Women Voters

The group of data above gives you *numbers,* not *percents.* How can you change the form of the data to answer the question?

EXAMPLE 1   Find the percent of residents registered to vote in 1998.

> **STEP 1**   Find the total number of residents in 1998.
>
> There were 3,500 residents. (the *whole*)
>
> **STEP 2**   Estimate how many people in the complex were registered to vote that year.
>
> There were about 1,400 registered voters. (the *part*)
>
> **STEP 3**   Divide the *part* by the *whole.*
>
> 1,400 ÷ 3,500 = 0.40 or **40%**

ANSWER: 40% of Johnson Public Housing residents were registered voters in 1990.

Math Recap
To find out what percent one number is of another number, divide the *part* by the *whole.*

EXAMPLE 2 Use the data shown on page 81 to find what percent of Johnson Public Housing residents were registered to vote in 1997.

     STEP 1 How many total residents are there?

        3,450

     STEP 2 How many registered voters are there?

        800

     STEP 3 Divide the part by the whole.

        $800 \div 3{,}450 = 0.2319$

     STEP 4 Change the decimal to a percent.

        $0.2319 = 23.19\%$

ANSWER: About 23% of Johnson Public Housing residents were registered to vote in 1997.

Why Change the Form of Data?

Why is it useful to see the data on page 81 changed to percent? The following activity will help you see why.

Compare the **number** of registered voters in 1999 to those in 2000. Did the number go up or down?

The number of registered voters in the Johnson Public Housing Complex **fell** from 1,600 in 1999 to 1,400 in 2000.

Why do you think this drop occurred? Put a check mark next to any reasons that seem sensible to you.

    fewer volunteers working to register people

    no appealing candidates for office in 2000

    apathy or resentment among residents

    other: _____

1. Use the data on page 81 to figure the *percents* of registered voters in the box below. Then plot the voters on the graph below.

(**Remember:** to find percent, divide the part (number of registered voters) by the whole (number of residents). Percents for 1997 and 1998 have been computed for you.)

```
1996:   1,200 ÷ 3,900 is about _____%
1997:   800 ÷ 3,450 is about 0.23, or 23%
1998:   1,400 ÷ 3,500 is 0.40, or 40%
1999:   1,600 ÷ 3,280 is about _____%
2000:   1,400 ÷ 2,500 is _____%
```

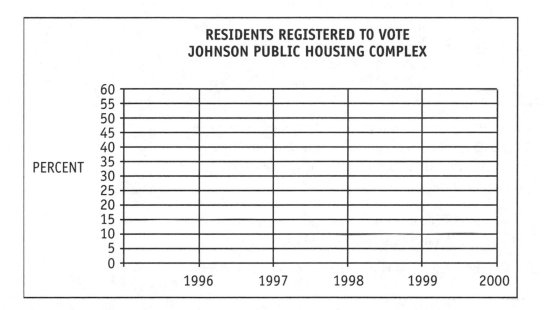

**RESIDENTS REGISTERED TO VOTE
JOHNSON PUBLIC HOUSING COMPLEX**

2. **a.** What happened to the percent of registered voters between 1999 and 2000? Did the percent rise or fall?

   b. Why do you think this happened?

Perhaps you already figured out that the number of registered voters fell because the total number of residents fell as well. But the percent of registered voters was greater than any other year!

Changing the form of data can help you see things that might not be obvious at first.

Here's another example of putting data into different forms.

Territory Sales Figures, 1999

Sales Representative	Region	Sales (in dollars)
David Burns	Northeast	$475,000
John Fay	South	290,000
Lisa Gagnon	Northeast	325,000
Kirsten Hutchinson	Northeast	190,000
Tamara Jenkins	South	315,000
Julio Kim	Midwest	219,000
Juanita Nalda	Midwest	220,000
Laura Rice	South	110,000
Rena Sanchez	South	328,000
Herm Thomas	Midwest	200,000
Raul Whitney	Northeast	150,000

Suppose you need to calculate a company's total dollars in sales for each region in 1999. The chart above contains the only data you have available to you. The chart is organized alphabetically by sales rep. Can you calculate total regional sales?

EXAMPLE Transform the data into a table that best summarizes the regional sales totals. A table has been started for you.

STEP 1 List the different regions in either a column or a row.

Northeast	
South	
Midwest	

or

Northeast	South	Midwest

STEP 2 Add up the sales figures for each region.

Northeast: 475 + 325 + 190 + 150 ($\times$ 1,000) = **1,140,000**
South: 290 + 315 + 110 + 328 ($\times$ 1,000) = **1,043,000**
Midwest: 219 + 220 + 200 ($\times$ 1,000) = **639,000**

STEP 3 Finish writing the totals in the appropriate column or row.

Although the original purpose of a set of data might be different from your purpose, changing the *form* of the data can often help you get the information you need.

Change the form of the data by following the steps indicated.

3. Use the steps below to find what *percent* of patients have each different insurance plan. Your information source is the graph below.

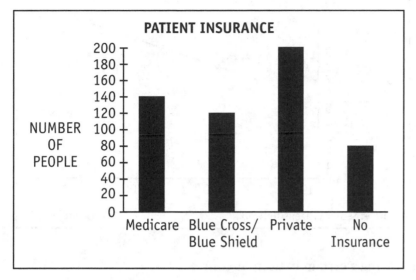

STEP 1 Find the total number of patients by adding up the numbers from each insurance category.

STEP 2 To find each percent, divide the *part* (each insurance category) by the *whole* (total patients).

STEP 3 Fill in the chart started below.

Insurance	Medicare	Blue Cross/ Blue Shield	Private	No Insurance
Percent of Patients				

4. An agency estimates that the total number of homeless people in Sun County is 9,500. Use this and the following information to find the *number* of homeless people that were counted in each area and add the information to the chart.
(0.37 × 9,500, and so on)

Sun County Homeless Population

Downtown Area	37% or _____
Central Square	29% or _____
East Side	22% or _____
West Side	10% or _____
Outlying	2% or _____

Seeing Trends/Making Predictions

What is a trend?
Do you see a trend on the graph at the right?

AVERAGE LENGTH OF RESIDENCE AT GLENDALE SENIOR CITZENS CENTER

YEARS

Source: Senior Citizens Network   * projected

A **trend** is a general movement following a certain pattern or course. To understand what a trend is, fill in the blanks.

- Between 1980 and 1990, the average length of residence at Glendale Senior Citizens Center rose by _____ years.

- Between 1990 and 2000, the average length rose by _____ years.

- Between 2000 and 2010, the average length is expected to rise by _____ years.

Did you notice something repeating? Every 10 years, the average length of residence goes up by 2 years. The graph above indicates a pattern, or *trend,* in average length of residence at Glendale Senior Citizens Center.

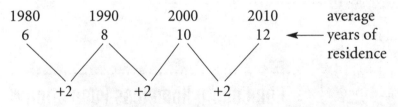

average years of residence

If the trend continues, what will the average length of residence be in the year 2020?

To answer the question, follow the trend by adding 2 years to the average length of residence in 2010.

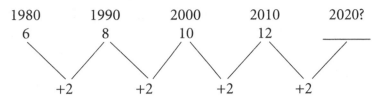

1980   1990   2000   2010   2020?
6   8   10   12   _____

+2   +2   +2   +2

The average length of residence in the year 2020 will be **14** (12 + 2), *if the trend continues.*

General Trends

The trend on the graph on page 86 showed a rise of exactly the same number of years every 10 years (or every decade). Sometimes trends are more general—they follow a pattern, but one that is not as simple as the trend you saw before. Look at an example.

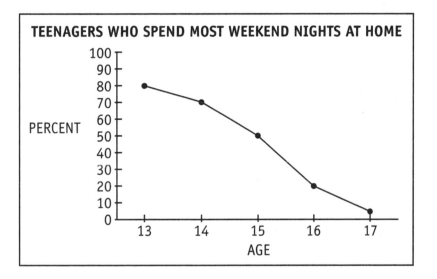

TEENAGERS WHO SPEND MOST WEEKEND NIGHTS AT HOME

PERCENT (y-axis: 0 to 100)

AGE (x-axis: 13, 14, 15, 16, 17)

Do you see a trend concerning teenagers who stay home most weekend nights?

As you can see, there is certainly a *downward* trend with increasing age, but the size of the drop is different at each jump in age.

If the trend continues, will the percent of 18-year-olds who stay at home most weekend nights be *higher* or *lower* than the percent of 17-year-olds?

You're right if you said **lower.** Although you cannot tell how much lower, you can see from the *general trend* of the data that the percent will go down.

Projected Data

Have you ever seen numbers in a newspaper or work report that are labeled **projected?** This label means that the data is not yet available. Instead, experts are making an estimate based on a trend. The chart shows *projections* of the world's population in the next three decades. These estimates are based on population totals measured in previous decades.

World Population*	
Year	**Population**
2000	6,291,000,000
2010	7,255,000,000
2020	8,281,000,000

*Projected
Source: U.S. Census Bureau

Use the data below to solve problems 1 and 2.

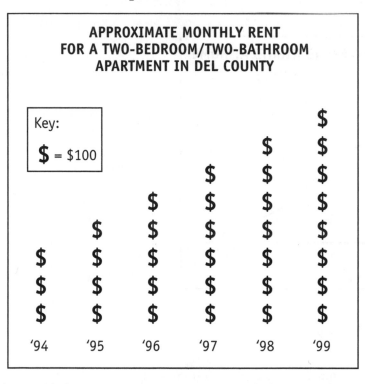

APPROXIMATE MONTHLY RENT FOR A TWO-BEDROOM/TWO-BATHROOM APARTMENT IN DEL COUNTY

Key: $ = $100

'94 '95 '96 '97 '98 '99

1. If the trend shown continues, approximately how much would the monthly rent for a two-bedroom/two-bathroom apartment be in 2000 in Del County?

2. Make a statement about the approximate monthly rent in 2001.

_____

_____

Use the list of phrases below to write four statements about the data displayed on the graph.

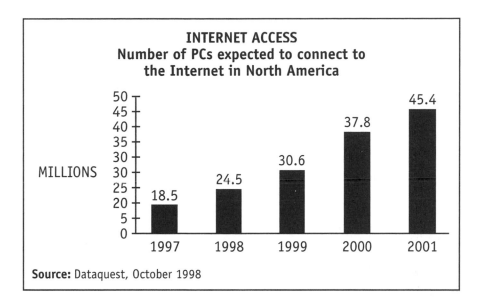

INTERNET ACCESS
Number of PCs expected to connect to the Internet in North America

MILLIONS

| | 18.5 | 24.5 | 30.6 | 37.8 | 45.4 |
| | 1997 | 1998 | 1999 | 2000 | 2001 |

Source: Dataquest, October 1998

if the trend continues	was less in 1999
rose steadily	approximately 7 million more
about 6 million fewer	is projected to be

EXAMPLE _The number of PCs expected to connect to the Internet in North America was less in 1999 than in 2000._

3. _____

_____

4. _____

_____

5. _____

_____

6. _____

_____

Group Project: Summarizing Your Data

Choose some of the data you collected and organized in the first two chapters and plan to summarize what you have discovered.

Write an article that answers *one* of the following questions, using your data as support for your ideas. Or, you may answer a question of your own if you prefer. In your article, be sure to

- summarize your data accurately
- use specific numbers or percents
- try showing your data in different forms
- notice trends
- use any other data or information you've found in books or newspapers

Questions

1. Do people who live alone tend to watch more television than those who live with others?

2. Are married people more often day people or night owls?

3. Do more people recycle glass or paper? How about aluminum?

4. Are people today satisfied with their president?

5. Do people with fewer close friends go out more or less often than people with more close friends? Which group watches more television?

6. Is the economy or the environment a bigger concern for people?

7. Who tends to have pets—married people or single people? Male or female?

8. What section of the newspaper is the most popular? Do more men than women read the sports first?

9. Who thinks Americans should buy only American products— people who are concerned about the economy or people who are concerned about the environment?

10. Summary: _____

_____

_____

_____

_____

_____

_____

_____

_____

_____

_____

_____

_____

_____

_____

_____

_____

_____

_____

_____

_____

_____

_____

_____

_____

USING PROBABILITY AND STATISTICS

What Are the Chances?

"I'll probably get put on the late shift at work," said Dan, a new employee. "Personnel told me that 9 out of 10 new people start out there."

Why does Dan think he'll be put on the late shift?
Is Dan *sure* what shift he'll be put on?

Probability is the chance that an event will occur. To picture probability, use coin tossing. Toss a coin in the air and let it fall. Is one side more likely to be faceup?

1. Toss a coin 10 times and record the number of heads and tails.

   First 10 tosses:
   Heads _____
   Tails _____

2. Now toss the coin 10 more times and again record the results.

   Second 10 tosses:
   Heads _____
   Tails _____

3. Write a statement about the total number of heads vs. the total number of tails.

   _____

   _____

You can show the results of the coin-tossing experiment as a fraction or as a ratio.

$$\frac{\text{number of times outcome occurred}}{\text{total number of outcomes}}$$

Using the information from above, write the fractions showing the number of tails and heads in *20* tosses.

$\dfrac{\square \quad \text{number of tails}}{20 \quad \text{total tosses}}$ $\qquad$ $\dfrac{\square \quad \text{number of heads}}{20 \quad \text{total tosses}}$

Fractions or ratios such as these can be used to *estimate the probability* of tossing either heads or tails. In fact, the more times you toss the coin and record the outcome, the closer you will come to knowing the actual probability. By now, you may realize that the chance of tossing heads (or tails) is close to $\frac{1}{2}$.

Here's how to represent probability.

$$\text{Probability of an event} = \frac{\text{number of desired outcomes}}{\text{total number of possible outcomes}}$$

In the case of the probability of tossing heads, the desired outcome is heads. Therefore, the probability of tossing heads is expressed as

$$\text{probability} = \frac{1}{2}$$ ← (because there is 1 head on the coin)
← (because there are 2 possible outcomes, heads or tails)

Go back and compare this fraction to the other fractions you have worked with in this experiment. What do you notice?

When you are dealing with coin tossing, all fractions and probabilities are very close to $\frac{1}{2}$.

You have learned that probability depends on the number of *desired outcomes* and the total number of *possible outcomes.*

When you roll a number cube, the chances are the same that any one of the numbers 1 to 6 will appear faceup.

EXAMPLE   What is the probability of rolling a 6?

$$\frac{1}{6}$$ ← (there is one 6 on the number cube)
← (number of sides on the number cube)

4. What is the probability of rolling a 1?

5. What is the probability of rolling an odd number?

6. What is the probability of rolling a number divisible by 3?

Now let's return to Dan's situation from the beginning of this lesson.

7. Write a fraction representing the probability that Dan will be put on the late shift.

8. What is the probability that Dan will *not* be put on the late shift?

Probabilities Between 1 and 0

What is the probability that you will fly to the moon tomorrow?
Express this probability as a fraction.

$\dfrac{0}{1}$ ← number of outcomes
  ← number of possible outcomes
(There's only one possibility: you won't go.)

The chances that I will fly to the moon tomorrow are 0.

What is the probability that tomorrow will follow today?

$\dfrac{1}{1}$ ← number of outcomes
  ← number of possible outcomes
(Tomorrow always follows today.)

It is virtually a sure thing that tomorrow will follow today. Therefore, you can express this probability as 1.

- A probability of 1: The event will certainly happen.

- A probability of 0: It's not possible for the event to occur.

- All other probabilities are expressed as fractions between 0 and 1, just as you learned in the last lesson.

Imagine that the numbered cards below are facedown on a table. You pick up one card, not knowing which one you are choosing.

1. What is the probability that the number on the card you chose is a 4?

2. What is the probability that the number on the card is greater than 3?

3. What is the probability that the number on the card is divisible by 2?

4. What is the probability that the number on the card is greater than 8?

Look at each of the following situations and circle whether it has a probability of 0 (no chances of occurring), 1 (a sure thing), or somewhere in between.

What are the chances that

5. you will eat a hamburger in the next year?

   0   in between   1

6. it will rain somewhere in the world today?

   0   in between   1

7. someone in your state will die tomorrow?

   0   in between   1

8. you will win a million dollars in the lottery?

   0   in between   1

9. a plane is taking off now?

   0   in between   1

10. we will have world peace tomorrow?

    0   in between   1

11. a woman is giving birth right this minute?

    0   in between   1

12. the sun is shining somewhere in the world?

    0   in between   1

13. everyone will be using public transportation by the year 2000?

    0   in between   1

14. the Cubs will win the World Series?

    0   in between   1

15. Write down three events that have a probability of 0. Use your imagination!

16. Write down three events that have a probability of 1. Be creative.

Using Data to Estimate Probability

Suppose you work in a Social Security office. A person who receives Social Security benefits approaches your desk.

What are the chances that this person is a retired worker?

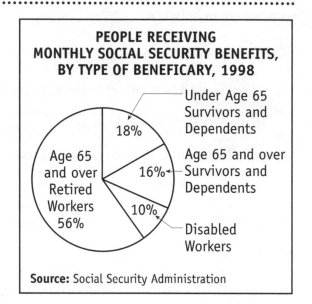

PEOPLE RECEIVING MONTHLY SOCIAL SECURITY BENEFITS, BY TYPE OF BENEFICARY, 1998

Under Age 65 Survivors and Dependents — 18%

Age 65 and over Survivors and Dependents — 16%

Disabled Workers — 10%

Age 65 and over Retired Workers 56%

Source: Social Security Administration

Look at the data at the right. The chances that a person who receives Social Security benefits is retired are pretty good—a little more than $\frac{3}{5}$ or 3 out of 5. How do you know this?

56% of people receiving benefits are retired.

$\underline{56}$ ← percent of retired people
100 ← total percent of people receiving benefits

Math Recap
Remember that 56% means 56 out of 100.

This relationship can also be expressed in terms of a probability.

$\frac{56}{100}$ is approximately equal to $\frac{60}{100}$ is equal to $\frac{30}{50}$ or $\frac{3}{5}$

Out of every 5 people receiving Social Security benefits, approximately 3 are retired.

Therefore, you can say that the chances are about 3 out of 5 that the person who approached your desk is a retired beneficiary.

What are the chances that the person who approached your desk is *not* a retired beneficiary?

1. According to the graph, what percent of people receiving benefits are *not* retired?

   $100\% - 56\% = \underline{\hspace{1.5cm}}$

2. Express this percent as fraction, estimate, and reduce.

   $$\frac{\boxed{}}{100} \approx \underline{\hspace{2cm}} = \underline{\hspace{1.5cm}}$$

   estimate   reduced

3. Express the fraction as a probability. The chances that a person receiving Social Security benefits is *not* a retired beneficiary are about _____.

(**Note:** Since you already know that the chances are 3 out of 5 that a person *is* a retired beneficiary, you could also subtract to find that the chances are 2 (5 − 3) out of 5 that a person is *not* a retired beneficiary.)

Does your statement sound something like this?

The chances that a person receiving Social Security benefits is not a retired beneficiary are **about 2 out of 5.**

How Can We Be Sure?

Can you correctly identify what type of beneficiary is approaching your desk simply by using probability?

No, you can't. Even if the chances are 9 out of 10 that a person is retired, you could never be sure that the person approaching your desk is not that 1 person out of 10 who *isn't* retired.

As you learned in the last two lessons, probability allows you to make *reasonable guesses,* not exact predictions.

For example, it is very hard to predict the outcome of one coin toss. (Will it come up heads or tails?) However, probability allows you to reasonably guess how many heads (or tails) would come up in 100 tosses.

Similarly, the data above cannot assure you that the person approaching your desk is a retired beneficiary. However, if 100 people receiving Social Security benefits approached your desk, you could make a reasonable guess that somewhere around 56 of them would be retired beneficiaries.

Use the data to determine the probabilities below.

EXAMPLE   What were the chances that in 1999 a
registered voter in Kensington County was
an independent?

	Registered Voters, Kensington County	
	1998	**1999**
Democrats	1,280	1,580
Republicans	960	820
Independents	320	600

STEP 1   How many 1999 registered voters were
there in all?

$$1{,}580 + 820 + 600 = 3{,}000$$

STEP 2   What fraction was registered
independent?

$$\frac{600}{3{,}000} = \frac{1}{5}$$

ANSWER: The chances that a voter registered as an independent in
Kensington County in 1999 are **1 out of 5.**

4.   What were the chances in 1998 that a voter registered in
Kensington County was a Democrat?

STEP 1   How many 1998 voters were there in all?

STEP 2   Write a fraction comparing the number of 1998
registered Democrats to all 1998 registered voters
in Kensington County. Reduce the fraction.

5.   What was the probability that a voter registered in Kensington
County in 1998 was *not* a Republican?

6.   What was the probability that a voter registered in Kensington
County in 1998 was an independent?

7.   Was the probability that a voter registered in Kensington County in
1999 was *not* a Democrat less than $\frac{1}{2}$ or greater than $\frac{1}{2}$?

8.   Were the chances that a voter in Kensington County in 1999 was a
registered Republican less than $\frac{1}{3}$ or greater than $\frac{1}{3}$?

An Introduction to Sampling

Advertising Executive: "We took a survey of 1,500 people, and 1,125 of them said that they did not like our chocolate french-fry idea. So we've decided not to sell them at all."

French-Fry-Loving Friend: "Just because 1,125 people out of this entire country don't like the idea doesn't mean the rest of us don't! Why don't you listen to us instead?"

How do you think a company decides whether or not a product will sell well?
What mistake is the friend making in his comment above?

To the french-fry lover, 1,125 people does not seem like a large number—especially since he compares the number to the population of the whole country! However, the company is actually comparing **1,125** to the **1,500** people it surveyed—not all 250 million people in the United States.

Use what you have learned about percents and probability to complete the following statements.

The chances that a person would not like chocolate-covered french fries are 1,125 out of _____, or 3 out of _____.

The percent of Americans who do not like the idea of chocolate-covered french fries is _____%.

In fact, based on the company's survey, the chance is **3 out of 4** that a person would not like chocolate-covered french fries—a total of **75%**. With so many people disliking the idea, the company was very wise not to go ahead and sell them.

But how can the company base its decision on the responses of 1,500 people? The company can use a **sample** of the population to predict how a larger group will respond.

Population and Sample

The study of statistics makes it possible to learn about a large group of people, places, or things (the **population**) by looking at information about a smaller part of that group (the **sample**). Look at some examples of how samples are used to make decisions and predictions every day in government, the business world, and even your own life.

EVERYDAY DATA

When choosing where to shop, people often compare prices in different stores. For example, suppose one store charges more for aspirin, paper products, toothpaste, and diapers. "This store has higher prices," you might say to yourself. "I'm not going to shop here." Based on a *sample* of prices, you made a decision about the prices in general, the *population*.

BUSINESS

A factory worker inspects a carton of light bulbs that has just been packed. She finds that 18 of the 240 bulbs are broken. "Something is wrong with the packing machine on this line," she says. "We'll need to recall all cartons that were packed today." Based on a *sample* of bulbs, the worker makes a prediction about what she'll find in all the cartons, the *population*.

GOVERNMENT

Government statistics indicate that population in California grew to thirty-two million in 1997. Did the government count each and every person living in California? Absolutely not. Instead, it chose a *sample* of the region, and based on how the population grew in that sample, it made an accurate estimate of the entire California *population*.

For each situation given below, write the population and the sample.

EXAMPLE   To predict the total number of votes cast for each presidential candidate, a television station interviews voters and collects a sample of their preferences for president.

Population: *total votes*   Sample: *voters interviewed*

1. An education official wants to know the standardized test scores for sixth-graders in his state. He looks at records from sixth-graders in six different towns in the state.

   Population: _____   Sample: _____

2. A candidate for mayor would like to find out how she is perceived among low-income residents in her city. She asks her staff to survey people living in city low-income housing units.

   Population: _____   Sample: _____

3. A shift supervisor counts defective aluminum canisters produced between 12:00 and 1:00 A.M. to discover how many defective canisters were produced on the entire early-morning shift.

   Population: _____   Sample: _____

4. A customer returns three poorly made toys to the same toy store and decides that none of the store's merchandise is of good quality.

   Population: _____   Sample: _____

5. A store that sells cookies offers free pieces of its chocolate chunk cookies to passersby. People who taste the cookies decide that all the baked goods in the store are delicious.

   Population: _____   Sample: _____

Random Samples

Optimistic Moviemaker: "I want to make a movie that will appeal to *everyone*—a real blockbuster. So, my partners and I interviewed more than 100 people, and the results were amazing. Over 95% of the people we interviewed wanted to see more horror movies—more violence, more monsters, more creepy stuff. It's obvious what kind of movie we should make!"

Money-Maker: "You didn't by any chance interview the 100 people leaving the 4 P.M. showing of that new horror picture downtown, did you?"

Optimistic Moviemaker: "Why, yes, we did. How did you know?"

> **What is the *population* being discussed above?**
> **What is the *sample?***
> **Do you think most Americans want to see more horror movies?**

To make accurate decisions and predictions based on statistics, you must use a sample that is **representative** of the population you want to learn about. Is this true of the sample taken above?

Put a check mark next to the categories of people *you* think would be likely to watch a weekday afternoon horror movie downtown.

Teenagers	City dwellers
Adults	Suburbanites
People who work during the day	People who like horror movies
People who do not work during the day	People who don't like horror movies

Did you find that the people the optimistic moviemaker interviewed were probably young people who were not working during the day and who generally like horror movies? The sample might include exceptions, but these would probably be the characteristics of most of the people interviewed.

What does this tell you about the sample chosen for the moviegoing population? Certainly, it was not representative of the public in general.

A representative group of Americans should include *at least*

- both males and females
- people of different ages
- people of different races and ethnic groups

- employed and unemployed people
- people from cities, suburbs, and rural areas
- poor, middle-class, and wealthy people

How Can We Get a Representative Sample?

There are different ways to obtain a representative sample of a population. The best-known and generally most accurate method is called **random sampling.**

Suppose you had a jar full of colored balls—some red, some blue, and some green—all exactly the same size. If you mixed them all up in the jar, closed your eyes, and pulled out a number of them, you would have a random sample of the balls in the jar. None of the balls is more likely to be pulled out than another.

A sample of a population is considered a random sample if each member of the population is equally likely to be chosen.

When a government, business, or organization wants information about a population, it uses random sampling to gather data. A population can be any group—not only adult humans. It can include

- all mammals living in Southeast Asia

- children under age five with the same flu virus

- graham crackers produced daily in New York State

Remember that *population* refers to *the group that you want information about.* To get this information, you look at a *random sample* within this population.

First find the population and the sample in each of the following situations. Then decide why each sample is *not* representative of the desired population.

1. A government official wants to find out what Americans think about cuts in the U.S. defense budget. He interviews 200 people outside a shopping mall in a small town near an army base.

   Population: _____   Sample: _____

   What is wrong with the sample? _____

   _____

2. A consumer wants to shop at the market with the freshest food. She reads the "date packed" label on whole chickens in five different stores.

   Population: _____   Sample: _____

   What is wrong with the sample? _____

   _____

3. "The people of the United States want a president who does not put a tax burden on people who have worked hard to achieve the American dream," says a candidate for office. The candidate's staff got this information from a survey of members of the American Small Business Owners Association.

   Population: _____   Sample: _____

   What is wrong with the sample? _____

   _____

4. A production worker inspects the first 100 circuit boards that are manufactured one Tuesday morning. She wants to know how many defective boards the manufacturer produces each month.

   Population: _____   Sample: _____

   What is wrong with the sample? _____

   _____

An Introduction to Surveys

- A candidate for public office wants to know whether or not the people in his state favor the death penalty.

- The personnel director at a large corporation wants to know if employees are happy in their jobs.

- A market research specialist wants to find out whether a company could make money manufacturing disposable socks.

What can these people do to get the information they need?

Government agencies, businesses, schools, political candidates, and nonprofit organizations are just some of the individuals and groups that conduct **surveys** or **polls** to obtain information. A *survey* or *poll* is a systematic collection of data from a random sample of a population.

Have you ever been involved in or heard about any surveys? What where they about? Have you ever phoned in your response to a televised survey question?

_____

_____

_____

Surveys are usually conducted in one of three ways. Take a look at how each works.

Put a check mark next to the survey you would be most likely to fill out and return for each survey category.

1. **Mail**

   Surveys by mail require you to fill out a questionnaire and mail it back to the sender.

   - Magazine music survey (favorite group, favorite song, and so forth)

   - Warranty and questionnaire that come with a product (stereo, appliance, and so forth)

   - Survey that comes with a cereal sample packet

   Would a self-addressed, stamped envelope or card influence your decision to respond to a survey? How?

2. **Telephone**

Currently, there are two types of telephone surveys. One type requires people to make a phone call to record their opinion (usually an 800 or 900 number). This kind of survey often appears on television shows.

The other type features a polling group or market researcher calling random phone numbers and asking questions.

- A polling group asking whom you are going to vote for in the next election

- A 900 number to call to show whether or not you support legalized abortion

- A market researcher calling to find out which household products you use

3. **Personal Interview**

Surveys are often conducted in person—in a shopping mall, on a street corner, or door to door.

- A survey conducted in a mall asking questions about you and your shopping habits

- A survey conducted on a street corner about what factors influence your choice of political candidates

- An official door-to-door census

Out of all the preceding choices, which survey would you be most likely to participate in? Why?

....

What do you think are the advantages and disadvantages of each type of survey?

1. Mail

Advantages: _____

_____

Disadvantages: _____

_____

2. Telephone

Advantages: _____

_____

Disadvantages: _____

_____

3. Personal Interview

Advantages: _____

_____

Disadvantages: _____

_____

Survey Organizations

You may already be familiar with the large survey and polling organizations in the United States. Here is a brief outline of some of them and what type of surveys they do.

PUBLIC OPINION POLLS

Major public opinion polling organizations include the *Gallup* poll, the *Roper* poll, and the *Harris* poll. These organizations survey people about their opinions in a wide range of areas, including politics, consumer products, and social issues.

They are highly respected organizations because they are *independent.* They do research and surveys on their own and sell their work to the media and other organizations that might be interested in reporting on it. These polling organizations provide objective data and statistics.

CURRENT POPULATION SURVEY

Like the U.S. Census, the *Current Population Survey* (or CPS) is a survey taken by the government, but it is taken *monthly,* not every ten years as is the census.

CPS is a survey of a random sample of 100,000 Americans, and it provides well-publicized information such as the unemployment rate, income statistics, and the birthrate.

NEWSPAPER AND NETWORK POLLS

Most major newspapers and television networks in the United States conduct surveys of their own.

Like Gallup, Roper, and Harris, the media also provide information about public opinion that they obtained from their own surveys.

4. Pick up a copy of a newspaper. Look for headlines and graphs that give statistics. Write down or cut out the headline, the date, the publication, the statistics, and *what polling or survey organization provided the statistics.*

Keep a journal of surveys and statistics over a period of time. This will provide an interesting year in review. It will also reinforce how frequently statistics are used.

Margin of Error

What do you think *margin of error* means in the chart at the right?

Percentage of Olson City Citizens That Have:	African Americans	Caucasians
Savings Accounts	65%	75%
Checking Accounts	70	80
Stocks/Mutual Funds	30	40
Savings Bonds	20	30

Margin of Error ±2%
Source: *Olson City Journal*

Many statistics include a statement of **margin of error.** This information tells the reader that the numbers may vary from the actual population. When information from a sample is applied to a whole population, some allowance must be made for possible differences between sample and population.

For example, when you consider the margin of error, the percent of Caucasian Olson City citizens who have checking accounts is determined this way.

percent reported
$$80\% - 2\% = 78\%$$
$$80\% + 2\% = 82\%$$

The percent of Caucasian Olson City citizens who have checking accounts is between 78% and 82%.

Use the data above to answer these questions.

1. What percent of African Americans in Olson City have savings bonds? _____%

2. Considering the margin of error, what is the range of African Americans owning savings bonds?

   20% − 2% = _____%

   20% + 2% = _____%

   The range is from _____% to _____%

More About Margin of Error

3. What can you say about the city council approval rating from March to April of 1999?

   _____

   _____

   _____

   _____

CITY COUNCIL APPROVAL RATINGS, JANUARY – JUNE 1999

PERCENT OF PEOPLE WHO APPROVE OF THE JOB THE CITY COUNCIL IS DOING

Source: *Daily Herald*   Margin of error: ±3%

4. What is the approval rating in March? _____%

5. What is the March approval rating adjusted for margin of error?

   from _____% to _____%

6. What is the approval rating in April? _____%

7. What is the April approval rating adjusted for margin of error?

   from _____% to _____%

8. Compare the low end of the range for March and the high end for April.

   March: _____% April: _____%

9. Is it possible that approval *rose* between the two months?   Yes No

   At first glance, you may decide that the approval rating went down between March and April. However, *it is possible that the approval rating for the city council actually rose a slight amount between these two months.*

Acceptable margins of error are 5% or less. Otherwise, the statistics are considered inaccurate. Margins of error can also be written in decimal form. For example, ±2% would be shown as ±0.02.

Margins of error are a good reminder that the reporting of statistics is not an exact science.

In a random sample from West Valley, 1,500 teenagers were asked the following questions. Here's how they responded.

	Yes	No	Don't Know
"Do you have a close relationship with your parents?"	22%	71%	7%
"Are you happier now than you were five years ago?"	39	46	15
"Do you think that most of your friends are happy?	35	55	10

Margin of error ±4%

Use the data above to answer the following questions.

10. What is the range of West Valley teenagers who do not have a close relationship with their parents?

    from ____% to ____%

11. Considering the margin of error, is it possible that more teenagers surveyed *are* happier now than five years ago? What are the ranges of possible percents?

12. How many teenagers surveyed said that most of their friends are happy?

13. How many teenagers surveyed answered "Don't know" to each question?

Group Project: Write Your Own Survey

In your first group project, you had a chance to conduct a survey that was already written for you. Now you'll have a chance to write and conduct your *own* survey.

STEP 1 What do you want to find out?

Your first step as a group is to choose a topic that interests you. Is there anything that you have been wanting to know about people in your class, neighborhood, town, or city? Here's your chance to learn more.

Remember that you can ask fact questions such as "Do you read the newspaper on a regular basis?" or opinion questions such as "Do you think our congressmen and congresswomen truly represent their constituents?" Choose a general topic to explore. It could be anything from gun control or the environment to restaurant preferences or favorite books.

Decide now as a group what you would like to learn more about from your survey and jot it down here:

_____

_____

STEP 2 Choose a population, sample, and survey method.

Remember that your population will be the group that you want information about. Is it your class? Your school? Your neighborhood? Neighborhood adults? U.S. citizens? Residents of your state?

Population: _____

Of course, you will not be able to select a true scientific random sample. For the purposes of this survey, your goal should be to survey as representative a group as possible. (**Remember:** A representative group means that each member of the population has an equal chance of being chosen for the sample.)

Decide as a group how you will choose your sample and the steps you will take to make sure your sample is random.

Sample: _____

Now decide how you will conduct your survey. Mail is probably not feasible for you as it is time-consuming and too expensive for this purpose. How about a telephone survey? Is this a good way to survey your population? Or should you try personal interviews? Will all members of your group or just some of you survey participants? Now is the time to decide.

Survey method: _____

STEP 3 Writing the questionnaire.

Here are some things to keep in mind as you write your survey questions.

- Ask straightforward, easy-to-understand questions. Questions that can be answered *yes* or *no* are easiest to tabulate.

- Try not to show bias in your questions. The person being asked the questions should not be able to detect your opinion on the issues.

- Keep the questionnaire short; it should not take longer than 5 or 6 minutes to answer all the survey questions.

- Test your questions on group members first. Replace or change the wording of any questions that are confusing.

Sample Questionnaire Format

	Yes	No
Question: _____	☐	☐
_____		
Question: _____	☐	☐
_____		
Question: _____	☐	☐
_____		
Question: _____	☐	☐
_____		
Question: _____	☐	☐
_____		

EVALUATING DATA

· ·

Do Statistics Lie?

Used Car Dealer: "Numbers don't lie, I'm showing you the selling prices of all eight cars sold off this lot in the past week. The car you're looking at is priced below all of them! This car is a great deal."

Customer: "How do I know these figures are true? You could be making them up."

Used Car Dealer: "Here's the printout from our computer. Check the selling prices for yourself."

Customer: "If you're telling the truth, this car is cheaper than anything you've sold lately. I'll take it."

> **Suppose the car dealer's numbers are accurate. What do they tell the customer about the car that's on the lot now?**
> **What conclusions is the customer jumping to using the data from the car dealer?**

The car dealer used a list of numbers, or data, to try to sell a used car. But should the data really convince the customer? What does the purchase price of other cars tell you about the quality and price of this *particular* car?

The data that the dealer uses might be accurate, but the **conclusion** the customer draws from the data is *not valid.*

> Accurate data and statistics don't lie, but be careful of how the numbers are interpreted.

In this chapter, you'll get a chance to see how accurate and reliable data can be misunderstood and misinterpreted.

The practice you now have in making statements about data will help you detect conclusions that are not valid.

Here's the data shown to the customer on page 114. Suppose the customer is deciding whether or not to buy a '95 Toyota Tercel for $8,040. Make two statements about the data. One statement should compare the price of the Tercel to the prices of these other cars.

1. The Tercel _____

_____

_____

_____

2. _____

_____

_____

_____

Car	Purchase Price
'97 Chevy Cavalier	$10,740
'98 Dodge Neon	8,385
'95 Mazda RX7	16,900
'98 Buick Regal	13,580
'96 Ford Taurus	8,075
'97 Honda Accord	11,685
'96 Honda Civic	9,250
'95 Ford Mustang	10,655

Your statements may sound similar to the ones below. Based on the data, were you able to say whether the Tercel is a good buy?

- The Tercel's price of $8,040 is lower than any other car price shown by the dealer.

- The purchase prices of the other cars range from $8,075 to $16,900.

The data cannot help you decide whether or not the Tercel is a good buy. All you can really conclude is that the Tercel is less expensive than any of the cars sold in the past week. As a consumer, you know that there is a lot more to buying a car (especially a used car) than comparing the price to the dealer's other prices!

This example shows that it is important not only to pay attention to statistics, but also to think about *how you interpret the statistics.*

3. **Critical Thinking** Was the car dealer lying? No. He provided accurate and truthful data. But was he being honest? Explain your reasoning.

Drawing Conclusions from Data

U.S. Leads World in Prison Use, a Survey Finds

WASHINGTON—By a widening margin, the U.S. remains the world's biggest user of prisons, a private research group reported.

"These statistics prove what I've been saying all along," said Paul. "Our legal system in the United States is the most efficient in the world. Just look at how many criminals our system arrests, convicts, and puts behind bars, compared to these other countries."

What do you think about Paul's statements?
Did he interpret the data accurately?
Do these statistics prove that the U.S. legal system is the most efficient in the world?

Number of People in Prison, per 100,000 Population—1990

Country	Prisoners per 100,000
United States	455
South Africa	311
Venezuela	177
Hungary	117
Canada	111
China	111

Source: *The Sentencing Project*

Write a statement that summarizes the purpose of the data above. Remember to include information about *what*, *when*, *where*, and *how*.

Statement: _____

_____

_____

Does your statement sound something like this?

The chart shows the number of people in prison in 1990, per 100,000 population, in six different countries.

At first, you may think Paul's statement makes sense. Maybe more prisoners do indicate more efficiency. But don't rely on just the numbers when you analyze Paul's statement! You need to use your thinking skills as well.

The data may be accurate, but the *conclusion* Paul draws from the data may not be accurate.

Asking yourself the following questions may help you draw other conclusions.

- What does it mean to have an "efficient legal system"? Does it mean that, when a crime is committed, the criminal is arrested, tried, convicted, and punished as swiftly and as inexpensively as possible?

- What information does this data give you about how many crimes are committed in the different countries and how quickly and inexpensively the criminals are imprisoned?

In fact, Paul's statement is not *proved* by the data. His statement is not necessarily untrue, but Paul needs other data to support his claim.

It is often difficult to decide whether or not someone's interpretation or conclusion is accurate. Always question how data is interpreted and what conclusions are being drawn.

Do not take it for granted that, if the numbers are accurate, any statement made *about* the numbers is accurate. *Your critical thinking skills are as important as the numbers.* The experience you now have in making statements about data will help you detect *invalid* conclusions.

The following two pages will allow you to practice using your thinking skills when analyzing data.

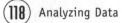

Each set of data below is accompanied by a statement that is not supported by the data.

    a. Write a short explanation telling why each interpretation is *not necessarily an accurate conclusion.*

    b. Then write a statement that is supported by the graph.

EXAMPLE   "Wow!" says Jeanette. "People in Watertown must get really dirty in August. Just look at how much soap they buy!"

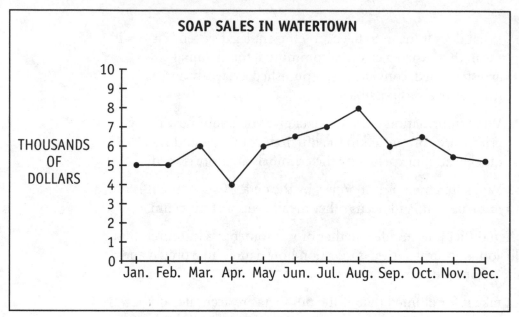

SOAP SALES IN WATERTOWN

THOUSANDS OF DOLLARS

    a. The fact that soap sales are high in August does not necessarily mean that people actually need more soap then or that they are dirtier.

    b. Soap sales in Watertown were highest in August and lowest in April.

1. "Numbers don't lie. Oral contraceptives are the best method for birth control if you don't want to be sterilized."

    a. _____

        _____

        _____

    b. _____

        _____

        _____

Failure Rates of Most Common Contraceptive Methods

Sterilization—less than 1%
Oral Contraceptives—6%
Condoms—16%
Diaphragms—18%

Source: Alan Guttmacher Institute.

2. "As the graph indicates, the citizens of North County pay far too much for police protection. Our police officers' salaries are the highest in five counties!"

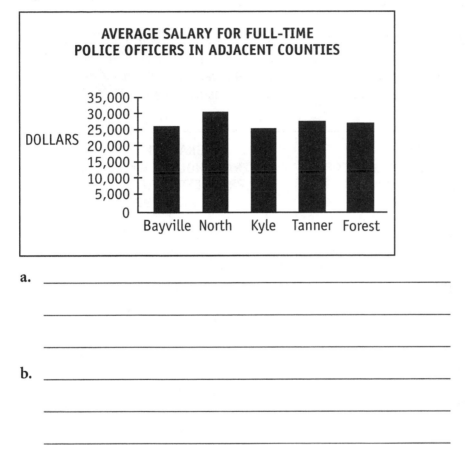

a. _____

_____

_____

b. _____

_____

_____

3. "Look at these statistics, Bob. It just goes to show you—our fire protection is not as great as you say it is."

a. _____

_____

_____

_____

_____

b. _____

_____

_____

Massachusetts Fire Deaths, 1997

Some Causes of Fire Deaths	Percent
Smoking	29
Electrical	27
Candle/Incense	9
Arson	7
Cooking	5

Source: Office of the State Fire Marshal, Stow, MA

Misinterpreting Graphs

Suppose you spoke to two job counselors.

First Counselor (Graph A): "As you can see from the graph, wages for production workers have been rising at a terrific rate. You'd be doing yourself a favor by getting into this field."

Second Counselor (Graph B): "The figures indicate that production wages are pretty flat. You might want to look into a field where wages are rising more quickly."

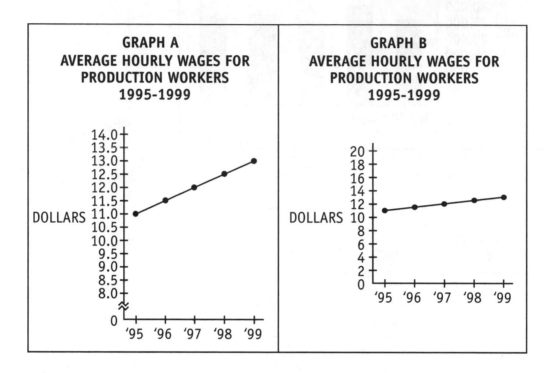

Which person is telling you the truth? Are they both reading the data correctly?
How can you make a decision based on two graphs that seem to be contradicting each other?

Fortunately, your work in this book and your own critical thinking skills will help you interpret graphs that might be misunderstood.

Make a statement summarizing Graph A. _____

_____

Does your statement hold true for Graph B?   Yes   No

Although Graph A seems to show a steady rise in wages and Graph B seems to show little rise, **both graphs actually present the same data.**

To see this clearly, fill in the blanks below. Use one graph to answer the question and the other graph to check your answer.

Between 1995 and 1999, production workers wages rose from about _____ per hour to about _____ per hour.

Both graphs show a rise from about **$11.00 to $13.00 per hour.**

If both graphs use the same data, why do the graphs look so different? The difference is in **scale.** Scale is the increase in value along the axis of a graph. As you learned in Organizing Data, the scale used to present data can vary. Sometimes the values on the scale can be multiples of 2, sometimes multiples of 5, 10, or 100.

The scale on Graph A increases by _____ at each interval.

The scale on Graph B increases by _____ at each interval.

With a smaller scale (increases of $0.50), the data line on Graph A rises higher to reach the $2.00 wage increase. With a larger scale (increases of $2.00), the data line does not need to rise very much at all.

In addition, compare the spacing between the dollar amounts on the scale of Graph A to the spacing of the dollar amounts on Graph B.

Which graph has larger spacing between the values on the vertical axis?

The spacing between the values on Graph A is greater than the spacing on Graph B. Therefore, the data line is steeper on Graph A.

So, how can you tell, by looking at the graphs, whether wages have increased a lot or a little?

You decide. You learned in Understanding Data that a number is neither small nor large until you compare it to another number. Neither Graph A nor Graph B will tell you whether $2.00 is a large increase. Understanding the data, collecting more information, and *using your thinking skills* will help you decide.

∙∙∙

Which of the following will help you decide whether a wage increase of $2.00 per hour is large or small? Circle Yes or No for each.

- the hourly wage increase in a related industry   Yes   No

- the number of jobs in the production industry   Yes   No

- the salary of a manager in the production industry   Yes   No

Did you decide that it would be useful to know how wages increased in related industries? If so, your thinking skills are right on target. Although you might be interested to know how many jobs are available and what a manager's salary is, these figures will not help you evaluate the $2.00 wage increase.

Your work in this lesson should help you keep in mind two important things.

1. *When analyzing data on a graph, pay close attention to the scale.* Don't look at just the shape of the data line. Use the skills you've developed in making statements about data to determine what is happening on the graph.

2. *Use your thinking skills.* Don't rely on what someone else says about the data. Find appropriate numbers to compare with the data. Use your judgment in deciding about the size of a figure.

Use the graphs and statements to answer the questions.

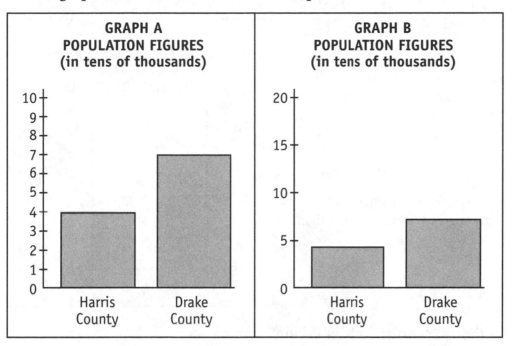

GRAPH A
POPULATION FIGURES
(in tens of thousands)

GRAPH B
POPULATION FIGURES
(in tens of thousands)

Statement 1: "The graph shows how much greater the population is in Drake County than in Harris County."

Statement 2: "As you can see, there's not a huge difference between Harris County and Drake County in terms of population."

1. Which statement do you think was made about Graph A? Which one was made about Graph B?

   a. Statement 1 refers to Graph _____.

   b. Statement 2 refers to Graph _____.

2. Make a statement comparing the population of Harris County with the population of Drake County.

   _____

   _____

3. Decide whether or not each of the following numbers would be useful in discovering if there is a big difference in population between the two counties. Circle Yes or No.

   Yes   No   a. the population figures for other counties in the state

   Yes   No   b. the number of people per square mile in each county

4. Write a paragraph describing the scale in each graph and how the scale influences the height of the data bars.

The Importance of Zero on a Scale

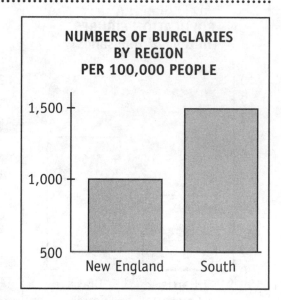

"Wow!" said Myra. "Look at this. The burglary rate in the South is about twice the rate in the Northeast. I didn't realize there was such a big difference."

Myra is correct that the bar showing the South's burglary rate *looks* about twice the height of the New England bar. But let's look at the data more carefully. Fill in the blanks below.

- There were _____ burglaries per 100,000 people in New England.

- There were _____ burglaries per 100,000 people in the South.

Is 1,500 twice as large as 1,000? Of course not. Then why does the graph make it appear that way?

The graph above may be misleading because it does not have a *zero* on the vertical scale. To see how important a zero is to the scale, compare the graph above to the one below—a graph that *does* include the zero.

As you can see, by including the full length of each bar (including the values between 0 and 500 that were left off the graph above), the graph pictures the correct proportion between 1,000 and 1,500.

It is important to look not just at the *picture* of the graph but also at the *labels* and *scale.* Beware of graphs that do not show a zero on the scale. Chances are that the proportions on the graph are misleading.

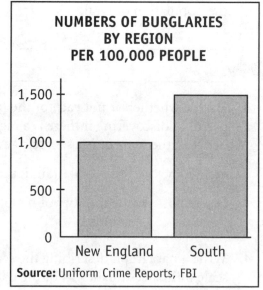

Zero Break

Sometimes you will see a graph that does show a zero on the scale, but then shows a *break* in the axis. The graph below is an example. A break like this is called a **zero break** or a **notch.**

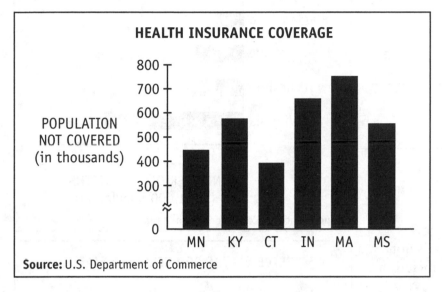

HEALTH INSURANCE COVERAGE

POPULATION NOT COVERED (in thousands)

800, 700, 600, 500, 400, 300, 0

MN KY CT IN MA MS

Source: U.S. Department of Commerce

Because all the data points to be included on the graph were above 300,000, the graph focuses on those values.

Is this graph misleading? Whenever you see a graph that includes a zero break, remember that the scale of the graph is different than it would be if all the values were included.

A graph showing a zero break is better than a graph that shows no zero on the scale at all.

To construct a graph using a zero break

STEP 1 Find the lowest and the highest values you will need to graph; mark these on the vertical axis.

For example, on the graph above, the lowest value to be graphed was about $400,000, and the highest was about $750,000.

STEP 2 Below the lowest value on the vertical axis, put a slash to indicate a break in the axis. Under the slash, write in a zero.

STEP 3 Finish graphing as usual.

Use the data for each problem to answer the questions.

1. "Live births in New Hampshire is half of live births in West Virginia according to this graph."

   Is this an accurate reading of the data? Why or why not? _____

   _____

   _____

   _____

   _____

   LIVE BIRTHS FOR SELECTED STATES

   Rhode Island

   Maine

   New Hampshire

   West Virginia

   10   15   20   25

   NUMBER OF LIVE BIRTHS
   (per 1,000 population)

   Source: National Center for Health Statistics

2. Redraw the graph so that it is not misleading. Remember to include a zero on the scale.

   LIVE BIRTHS FOR SELECTED STATES

   Rhode Island

   Maine

   New Hampshire

   West Virginia

   Source: National Center for Health Statistics

3. Use the data below to construct a line graph. Use a zero break between 0 and 25.

   Average Points per Game
   NBA Scoring Leader
   Michael Jordan

1991–92:	30.1
1992–93:	32.6
1994–95:	26.9
1995–96:	30.4
1996–97:	29.6
1997–98:	28.7

   AVERAGE POINTS PER GAME
   MICHAEL JORDAN

   AVERAGE POINTS PER GAME

   33
   32
   31

   0
   91–92

Understanding Correlation

Think back to what you learned about scatter diagrams in Organizing Data. Is there a correlation between hours spent watching TV and hours of free time?

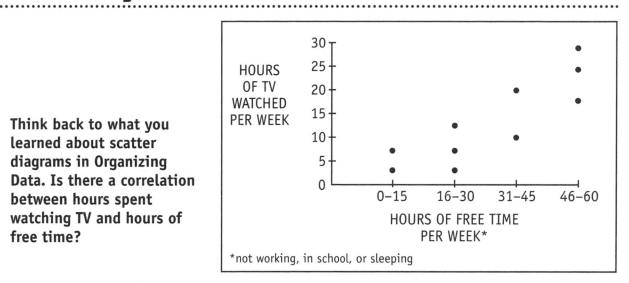

The scatter diagram above shows that there *is* a **correlation** between the two values graphed. As the number of hours of free time increases, so does the number of hours spent watching TV.

EXAMPLE 1 People with 25 hours of free time per week watch _____

(fewer, more)

hours of television than people with 10 hours of free time.

You should have written **more** in the space above.

The relationship shown above is a **positive correlation** because as one value rises, the other rises. To show correlation on a scatter diagram, a diagonal line is often drawn to show how most values cluster in a general pattern.

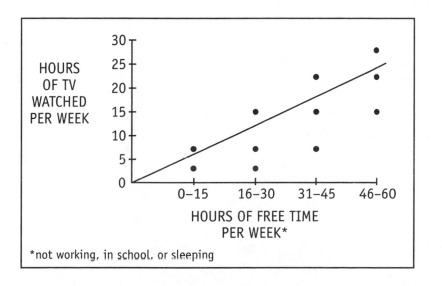

Another kind of correlation is a **negative correlation.** In this relationship, as one value rises, the other falls. Let's look at an example.

EXAMPLE 2 A manager in an appliance store did some research into portable headset sales and plotted the data on this scatter diagram. *Add the data in the chart to the diagram.* Other data has already been plotted on the diagram.

Price of Headset	Number of Headsets Sold
$45	10
40	10
35	21
30	22
25	40
20	40

What is the relationship between the two values on the diagram?

As the price of the headsets _____, the
　　　　　　　　　　　　　　　　　(rose, fell)

number of headsets sold _____.
　　　　　　　　　　　　　　　(rose, fell)

Did you write **fell** in the first blank and **rose** in the second blank? It is also true that as the price of the headsets rose, the number of headsets sold fell.

There is a correlation between the price of stereo headsets and the number sold; it is a negative correlation.

As you learned in Organizing Data, some values may not follow the pattern. Remember that a correlation can exist even if a few data points do not fall within the pattern.

Correlation vs. Cause

A recent consumer survey produced the data at the right.

"Hey, look at this," said Kathleen. "The more often people eat out, the more often they go to see a doctor. Information like this makes you never want to eat in another restaurant!"

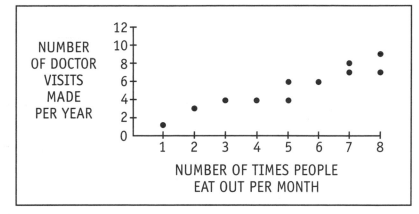

Is there a correlation between the number of times people eat out and the number of doctors' visits they make?
Which of the following do you think is the cause?

- **Frequently eating in a restaurant *causes* people to see a doctor more often.**

- **More frequent doctor visits *cause* people to eat out more.**

- **Neither of the above.**

Actually, although there is a correlation between these two values, neither one is the **cause** of the other. Kathleen jumped to a faulty conclusion when she analyzed the data. She did not understand that **correlation** is not the same thing as **cause.**

If eating in restaurants does not cause more frequent visits to the doctor, why does this correlation exist?

In fact, trips to the doctor and trips to a restaurant increase as a third value increases—income. The more money people make, the more they eat out in restaurants and go to the doctor. People with less money tend not to seek frequent medical care or eat out often because of the expense.

Sometimes, though, when there is a correlation between two values, one *can* be the cause of the other. In other words, one value can **have an effect on** the other value.

....

1. **Critical Thinking**   There is a negative correlation between a person's chances of being murdered and his or her income. In other words, the lower a person's income, the more likely he or she will be murdered. Why do you think this is so?

Circle the value that has an effect on the other value in each of the following correlations.

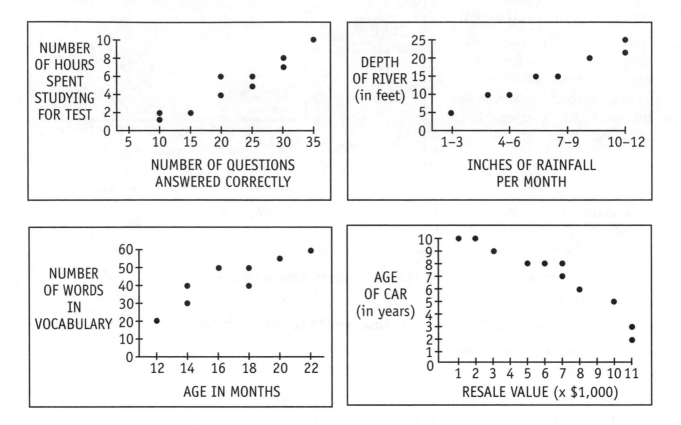

You should have found that

> **The number of hours spent studying** had an effect on the number of right answers.
>
> **The amount of rainfall** had an effect on the depth of the river.
>
> **Age** had an effect on vocabulary.
>
> **The age of a car** had an effect on its resale value.

These four examples show a causal relationship between values. Remember, however, that *not all correlations show causation* (cause).

Use the data below to answer the questions that follow.

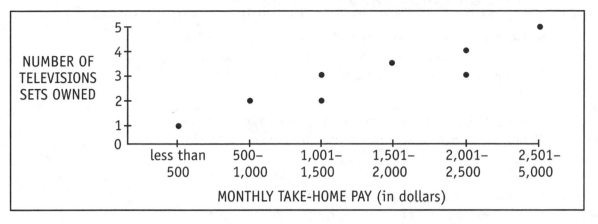

2. **a.** There is/is not a correlation between
    _____ and _____.

    b. "Now that I've seen these figures, I'm going to go out and buy another television set! My income is sure to go up."

    Is the analysis accurate? Why or why not?

    _____

3. **a.** As the number of school years completed _____, the

    number of hours spent reading per week _____.

    b. There is a _____ correlation between school years
    completed and time spent reading.

Bias in Surveys and Statistics

Jean: "This newspaper article says that over 60% of Americans approve of using our armed forces in the growing conflict overseas. That's 3 out of every 5 people! With a majority like that, I can't blame Congress for voting the way it did."

Roberto: "That's funny. A flier someone handed me on my way to work said that almost 80% of Americans did *not* approve of getting involved in the war. What's going on?"

Have you ever come across conflicting statistics? How can two sources like the ones above give such differing figures?

As you learned, some survey organizations are **independent** groups; in other words, they have no financial or political interest in their survey results. In general, their methods are respected and accurate.

Some surveys, however, are not as reliable. On page 102, you saw the inaccurate results of a survey conducted with a "nonrandom" sample—the horror movie-goers. Even though a group may intend to conduct a fair survey, flawed methods likely produce inaccurate statistics.

In addition, some polling groups have a **bias** concerning the outcome of a survey. In other words, they have a **preference** as to how people respond to questions on the survey.

If a survey's results appear to contradict other statistics, it is a good idea to look at the **source**—the group that gathered and analyzed the data. Ask yourself whether the source might benefit from people believing its survey results.

Suppose that the figures on the flier Roberto received were compiled by one of the groups below. Circle the group you think provided the statistics.

People for Peace, an organization that lobbies heavily against armed force involvement

Make America #1, a group that promotes the use of U.S. military power in conflicts worldwide

People for Peace would probably benefit if you believed that almost 80% of Americans were against getting involved in the war. These statistics support its cause. Make America #1 would probably have no interest in reporting that 80% of Americans did not support its point of view.

Of course, People for Peace may be reporting valid and accurate statistics. You simply cannot tell just by looking at them. However, if a source shows the possibility of bias, it is a good idea to find statistics from other sources to compare.

· ·

1. **Critical Thinking** Suppose the statistics on Roberto's flier came from an independent polling agency. Would you be more likely to believe them? Why?

Put a check mark next to each survey conducted that you think might show bias. Ask yourself if the people conducting the survey might have a preference for what the survey results showed.

2. A group called Citizens for Smith conducts a survey to find out how many people plan to vote for Smith in the city council election.

3. A soft-drink company reports a survey revealing which brand of soft drink teenagers prefer.

4. Americans Tough on Criminals surveys crime victims on their views concerning capital punishment.

5. A newspaper polls local communities to find out how they feel about gun control.

6. An inventor, trying to get financial support for her idea, does a survey asking people if they would buy a computerized laundry basket.

7. A television network conducts an exit poll outside a voting center to project the winners in an election.

Biased Methods

How might an organization go about gathering statistics that support its point of view? To be sure of getting the *right* responses, the polling group could use several different methods. Let's take a look at a couple of them.

SAMPLE BIAS

To obtain the results it wants, a group could survey only certain people—people who are likely to have the same point of view as the survey group. You saw an example of sample bias on page 102 in the survey of moviegoers. Sample bias is sometimes done intentionally and at other times by mistake.

As you do the activity below, remember that Make America #1 is the organization that promotes the use of military power.

....

Which of the groups below would Make America #1 most likely want to survey to find support for its cause?

a community with a large military base

a university town known for its antiwar demonstrations

You probably know that the first community would be the best choice for Make America #1. Although not *everyone* in the first community would be in favor of military involvement, there would certainly be a higher percent there than in the second group!

This example demonstrates the importance of a **random sample.** Almost any organization can find and survey a group that is known to support its positions. However, the statistics obtained would not necessarily reflect the opinion of most people.

Statistics are often accompanied by an explanation of the random sample and how it was obtained. If you suspect that the statistics are not based on a random sample, you should consider the possibility of bias and look for other sources and studies on the same topic before drawing conclusions.

QUESTION BIAS

Another way that survey groups can affect the outcome of their polls is by asking leading, or loaded, questions. This is called **question bias.** The wording of this type of question actually *directs* the respondent to answer in a certain way.

Go back and read the dialogue between Jean and Roberto on page 132. Both statistics have something to do with military involvement, but are they really contradicting each other?

Suppose the 60% quoted in Jean's article answered yes to the following question:

Do you approve of using our armed forces in the growing conflict overseas as a peacekeeping force to protect the innocent citizens of both countries?

And suppose that the 80% quoted in Roberto's flier answered no to this question:

Do you approve of getting involved in the war overseas by sending in armed American troops to fight in the battles of other countries?

There is a big difference in the numbers quoted because there is a big difference in the questions asked.

In addition, many survey questions are designed so that the person answering the question must choose from a multiple-choice format. But what happens if a person's true opinion is not listed as one of the choices? Many times, the answers recorded in a survey are not an accurate representation of people's true opinions.

· ·

8. **Critical Thinking**   Circle Yes or No to the following questions.

   Are taxes a good thing?   Yes   No

   Is America a free country?   Yes   No

   Are Americans hard-working people?   Yes   No

   You may have found yourself wanting to answer "not always" or "yes, but . . ." Can you see that yes/no type questions often do not allow you to express your true opinion?

The two organizations below surveyed people concerning their opinions on the U.S. space program.

Each group asked a loaded question to get a response that matched its own point of view. Match the organization to the question you think it would ask.

Space Is Our Future supports increased spending for space exploration.

"Are you tired of our government spending millions of dollars on useless efforts in space exploration while our own air, water, and plant life on Earth is in jeopardy?"

Home Earth seeks to divert government funds from space exploration toward environmental programs here on Earth.

"Do you believe that our government should put more resources into vital technological advancements such as space exploration so as to maintain our scientific superiority in the world?"

Did you match Space is Our Future with the second question and Home Earth with the first question?

Can you see how it would be difficult to answer no to either of these questions? The wording of each question leads us to answer yes. The survey statistics obtained from the responses to these two questions would be very different, wouldn't they? By using biased questions, each group could claim support for its own position.

....

Decide if each of the following survey situations is biased or unbiased. Write a brief explanation telling why.

9. To find out how city residents felt about a new factory being built in the midst of a large neighborhood, the chairman of Citizens for Economic Development asked, "Do you agree that new jobs and more taxpaying industry are important developments in this area of economic frailty?"

   biased   or   unbiased

   Why? _____

   _____

   _____

10. A television network surveyed people to find out what percent planned to vote in an upcoming presidential election.

    biased   or   unbiased

    Why? _____

    _____

    _____

11. To find out how city residents felt about a new factory being built in the midst of a large neighborhood, a group called Save Our Homes asked, "Are you willing to sacrifice your homes and community to a factory that will destroy the environment?"

    biased   or   unbiased

    Why? _____

    _____

    _____

12. A researcher surveyed people outside an exclusive shopping mall to find out how Americans were affected by the current recession.

    biased   or   unbiased

    Why? _____

    _____

    _____

13. A consumer opinion researcher stopped people coming out of an ice cream parlor and asked them what their favorite dessert was.

    biased   or   unbiased

    Why? _____

    _____

    _____

Critical Thinking with Data

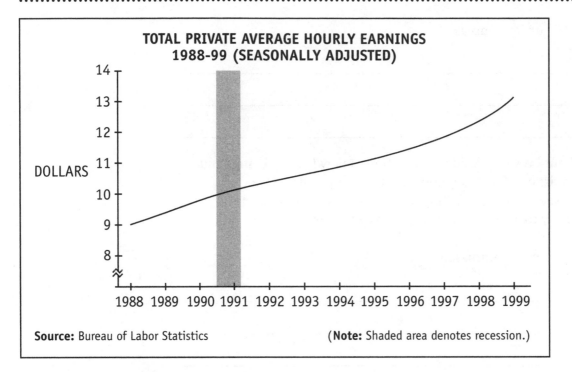

TOTAL PRIVATE AVERAGE HOURLY EARNINGS 1988-99 (SEASONALLY ADJUSTED)

DOLLARS

Source: Bureau of Labor Statistics   (**Note:** Shaded area denotes recession.)

Circle the statement(s) that are true based on the graph above.
- **Statement 1:** Average hourly earnings have gone steadily up between 1988 and 1999 due to an increase in skilled workers.
- **Statement 2:** There has been a huge increase in average hourly earnings between 1988 and 1999.
- **Statement 3:** During the 1990s, the U.S. economy was very healthy.
- **Statement 4:** Private average hourly earnings rose throughout the nineties.

An analysis or interpretation often accompanies data. Don't *assume* the analysis is accurate—use your **critical thinking** skills to see if the analysis is supported by the data.

At first, each statement above might appear true based on the graph. Let's find out why only statement 4 is actually based on the data provided.

For each statement, think about these questions.
- Is anything missing?
- Can the data be interpreted differently?
  Statement 1: Average hourly earnings have gone steadily up between 1988 and 1999 due to an increase in skilled workers.

Is anything missing? Yes, the graph gives no information about the causes of the increase. You do not know if an increase in skilled workers was the cause.

Remember: Even if you believe the statement to be true, the question asks which statements are *supported by the graph,* not which ones are true based on your prior knowledge or opinion.

Statement 2: There has been a huge increase in average hourly earnings between 1988 and 1989.

Can the data be interpreted differently? How? (**Hint:** What does *huge* mean?)

_____

_____

_____

The graph shows clearly that there was an increase in hourly earnings in the 1990s. But how can you decide whether this growth was "huge"?

In Understanding Data, you learned to compare numbers. You learned that a number is neither small nor large *until you compare it to another number.* In the example, what is the earnings increase being compared to? Earnings increases in the 1970s? Earnings increases in Japan?

Statement 3: During the 1990s, the U.S. economy was very healthy.

Is anything missing? Can the data be interpreted differently?

_____

_____

A healthy economy depends on more than earnings. To allow you to make a statement like this, the graph would need to show data concerning the inflation rate, the unemployment rate, gross national product, and other data.

Statement 4: Private average hourly earnings rose throughout the nineties.

This statement is true based on only the data provided on the graph.

Let's look at another example. Circle the statement(s) that are true based on the graph.

- **Statement 1:** In 1989 African Americans living in Queens, New York, were as wealthy as Caucasians.

- **Statement 2:** In 1989 median income for both African Americans and Caucasian households in Queens, New York, was about $33,000.

- **Statement 3:** Due to the success of affirmative action, African Americans in Queens are finally nearing economic equality with Caucasians.

- **Statement 4:** The rising median income among African American households in Queens, New York, is an example of the progress being made by African Americans nationwide.

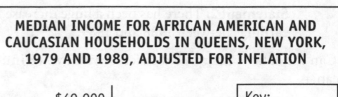

MEDIAN INCOME FOR AFRICAN AMERICAN AND CAUCASIAN HOUSEHOLDS IN QUEENS, NEW YORK, 1979 AND 1989, ADJUSTED FOR INFLATION

Source: U.S. Census Bureau

Statement 2 is the only statement that can be made based on the graph.

Let's look at the other statements more closely.

Statement 1 is too general. Income is only one indicator of wealth. We do not know the savings, real estate holdings, or other assets of the households shown.

Statement 3 cannot be made based on the graph because the graph gives no *reasons* for an increasing median household income among African Americans.

Statement 4 cannot be made based on the graph. What happens in one city does not necessarily reflect what is happening in other cities across the country.

Answer the questions using the graph below.

1. Make a statement about the number of Boston youth homicides by firearm during the 1990s.

   _____

   _____

   _____

   _____

   _____

2. Which of the following statements can be made based on the graph?

   a. No youths were killed by firearm in Boston through March of 1999.

   b. The number of Boston youth homicides by firearm in 1997 was less than one-third the number in 1993.

   c. More Boston youths are killed by firearm each year than any other accident.

   d. The number of youths killed by firearm in Boston has steadily declined since 1990.

Group Project: A Closer Look at Surveys

Take a look at this survey description and questionnaire. Discuss the survey with your group. Use the information you have gained in this book to help you decide whether or not it is a fair survey.

In September of 1999, Conservatives for America announced the results of a poll of Americans nationwide. A sample of 500 people were asked their opinions about the political process in the United States. Survey participants were chosen randomly from a list of homeowners in the greater Washington, D.C., area.

Question: Do you think the liberal media unfairly influence voter opinion?   Yes   No

Question: Do you agree with most people that special-interest groups have too much power in government?   Yes   No

Question: Given the huge increase in government social program spending over the past year, do you feel that it is time for citizens to start paying their own bills?   Yes   No

Question: Do you make large contributions to any political organization?   Yes   No

Now look at the analysis of this survey. Can your group design a better survey and rewrite the questions?

The date a survey is made can often influence its outcome. For example, September 1999 was only a short time away from a presidential election. People's opinions might be different then than in a nonelection year, for example.

Beware of questions that influence the respondent to be included in a group; many people are unwilling to go against a majority.

Questions should be specific; some people may think a $10 contribution is large, whereas others might feel that anything under $100 is small.

In September of 1999, Conservatives for America announced the results of a poll of Americans nationwide. A sample of 500 people were asked their opinions about the political process in the United States. Survey participants were chosen randomly from a list of homeowners in the greater Washington, D.C., area.

Question: Do you think the liberal media unfairly influence voter opinion?   Yes   No

Question: Do you agree with most people that special-interest groups have too much power in government?   Yes   No

Question: Given the huge increase in government social program spending over the past year, do you feel that it is time for citizens to start paying their own bills?   Yes   No

Question: Do you make large contributions to any political organization?   Yes   No

Do you think this group might have an interest in the outcome of the survey?

Are homeowners a representative sample of Americans?

Adjectives and adverbs can influence responses.

Questions like this one precede the actual question with a negative comment, thereby leading the respondent to a particular response.

Now go back to the survey your group wrote on pages 112–113.

Check your questions for any evidence of bias, using the sample survey as guidance. Then rewrite your questionnaire.

Posttest A

This posttest gives you a chance to check your skill at data analysis. Take your time and work each problem carefully. When you finish, check your answers in the back of the book and review any topics on which you need more work.

For problems 1–3, refer to the following data.

Davco, Incorporated

Department	Number of Employees Who Carpool to Work	Number Employees Who Take Public Transportation	Total Number of Employees in Department
Sales	26	55	110
Service	10	10	25
Administrative Pool	15	12	30
Maintenance	10	6	18
Management	1	5	20

1. Which of the departments, sales or service, has the higher *rate* of employees who carpool to work?

2. According to the chart, about 30% of Davco employees carpool to work. What numbers can you compare with this figure in order to decide if 30% is a large number or a small number?

   a. the total number of employees
   b. the percent of people who carpool to other nearby industries
   c. the number of cars in the company parking lot

3. Write a statement about the number of management employees who carpool to work compared to the number of maintenance workers who carpool.

For problems 4–7, refer to the following data.

NEW ONE-FAMILY HOUSES SOLD IN THE U.S.
Seasonally Adjusted Annual Rate

Source: U.S. Census Bureau

4. Which of the following best summarizes the graph?

   a. The graph shows new one-family house sales in the U.S. from 1994 to 1999 in thousands of units.
   b. The graph shows the rise in housing costs in the U.S. from 1994 to 1999.
   c. The graph shows new home sales in the U.S.

5. What is the range of units provided on this graph?

6. Use the data to make a statement comparing new one-family home sales for two different years.

7. Which statement about the graph is *not* true?

   a. The number of new one-family homes sold in the U.S. in October 1998 was higher than in January 1999.
   b. About 600,000 new one-family houses were sold in the U.S. in January 1994.
   c. January 1995 was the month in which the fewest new one-family homes were sold in the U.S. between 1994 and 1999.

For problems 8–11, refer to the following newspaper article.

According to a recent survey, over 70% of Americans would rather eat a baked potato than rice at mealtimes, and 20% actually eat potatoes for breakfast. At the annual Potato Lovers Picnic in Daisy County last year, almost 750 pounds of potatoes were consumed by the 3,000 participants there. A spokesman for the event reported that potato sales are up 5% in the county from last year's sales figure of $940,000.

8. Which of the following organizations would most likely benefit from biased statistics in the survey above?

    a. WXYZ television news
    b. American Food Industry, Inc.
    c. American Potato Growers, Inc.

9. To ensure that people say that they prefer potatoes to rice, which of the following questions might the survey group ask?

    a. Would you prefer a hot, buttered baked potato or a bowl of rice?
    b. Which do you prefer to eat: a baked potato or rice?
    c. Which do you have more often at mealtimes: a baked potato or rice?

10. Which of the following would be a biased sample on which to conduct the potato-or-rice survey?

    a. 1,000 people working in a city government building
    b. 500 people leaving a professional baseball game
    c. 3,000 participants at the Potato Lovers Picnic

11. According to the survey, what are the chances that an American will eat potatoes for breakfast?

For problems 12–14, refer to the following data.

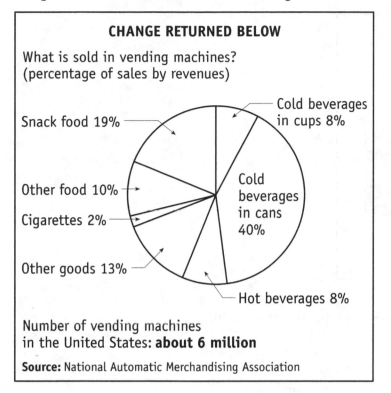

CHANGE RETURNED BELOW

What is sold in vending machines?
(percentage of sales by revenues)

Snack food 19%

Cold beverages
in cups 8%

Other food 10%

Cold
beverages
in cans
40%

Cigarettes 2%

Other goods 13%

Hot beverages 8%

Number of vending machines
in the United States: **about 6 million**

Source: National Automatic Merchandising Association

12. Which category of vending machine sales had the greatest percent?

13. What is the purpose of the graph above?
   a. to show how much change people receive from vending machines
   b. to show the rising cost of snack foods sold in vending machines
   c. to show percentage of vending machine sales for different categories

14. Use the graph to write a statement about vending machine sales.

For problems 15–18, refer to the following data.

NUMBER OF WORKERS
WHO WORKED AT HOME: 1960-1990

4,663,000

2,685,000

2,178,000

3,406,000

1960   1970   1980   1990

Source: U.S. Census Bureau

15. How many more home workers were there in 1990 than in 1980?

16. Which of the following statements summarizes the data?

   a. The graph shows the number of workers who worked at home in 1990.
   b. The graph shows the percent of workers who worked at home between 1960 and 1990.
   c. The graph shows the number of workers who worked at home between 1960 and 1990.

17. Use the graph to write a statement comparing two years.

18. Which of the following statements is *not* true according to the graph?

   a. In 1960 fewer than 5,000,000 workers worked at home.
   b. In 1980 fewer workers worked at home than did in 1970.
   c. In 1960 more workers worked at home than in an office or place of business.

For problems 19–22, refer to the following data.

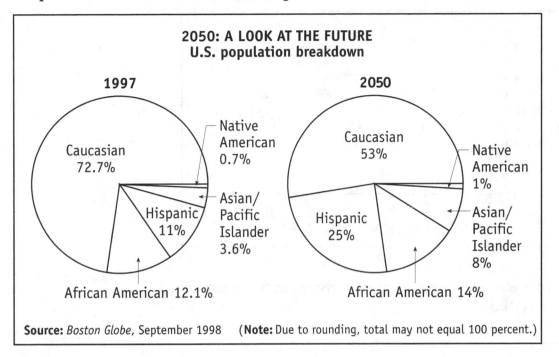

2050: A LOOK AT THE FUTURE
U.S. population breakdown

1997

Caucasian 72.7%

Native American 0.7%

Asian/ Pacific Islander 3.6%

Hispanic 11%

African American 12.1%

2050

Caucasian 53%

Native American 1%

Asian/ Pacific Islander 8%

Hispanic 25%

African American 14%

Source: *Boston Globe*, September 1998   (**Note:** Due to rounding, total may not equal 100 percent.)

19. What percent of the 1997 U.S. population was Hispanic?

20. Which of the following statements best summarizes the data of both graphs?

    a. There are more Caucasians in the U.S. now than ever before.
    b. The percentage of Caucasians in the U.S. is projected to decrease, while the percentages of minorities will increase.
    c. As the percentage of Caucasians in the U.S. decreases to 50%, so too will the overall U.S. population.

21. Write a statement about the population of the U.S. in the future.

22. Use data from both graphs to *estimate* the percent of the U.S. population that will be African American in the year 2020.

For problems 23–25, refer to the following data.

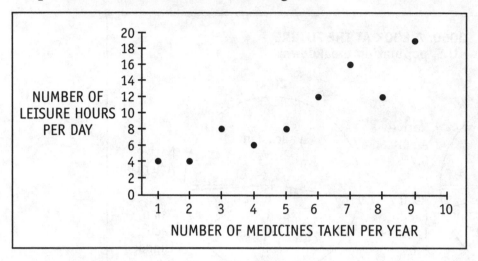

23. Is there a correlation between number of leisure hours and number of medicines taken?

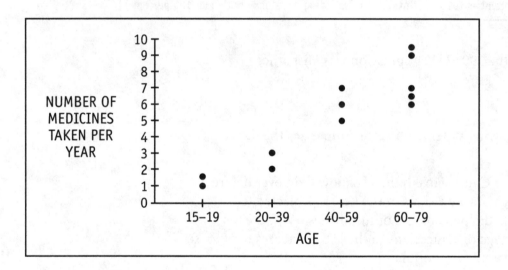

24. Is there a positive or a negative correlation between age and number of medicines taken?

25. Write a short summary of the data above. Do you think any of the three factors listed (age, leisure time, number of medicines taken) has an effect on the other factors?

For problems 26–28, refer to the following data.

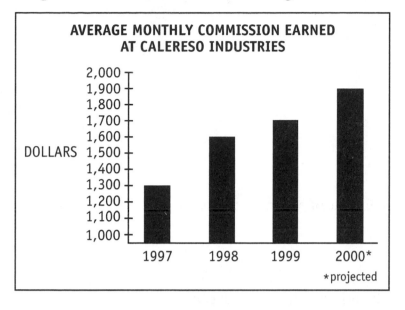

AVERAGE MONTHLY COMMISSION EARNED AT CALERESO INDUSTRIES

26. Write a statement about average monthly commission at Calereso Industries in 2000.

27. Which of the following statements is true according to the graph?

   a. The average monthly commission at Calereso will exceed $2,000 in 2001.
   b. The average monthly commission at Calereso was twice as high in 1998 as in 1997.
   c. The average monthly commission at Calereso rose steadily between 1997 and 1999.

28. Was the average monthly commission earned in 1999 twice the amount earned in 1997? Why does it appear that way on the graph?

For problems 29–32, refer to the following data.

Projected Election Results	
Crane	46%
Davidson	39%
Thurman	10%
Rizzo	5%

Margin of error ± 4%

29. Given the margin of error, what is the range of percent of projected votes received by Thurman?

30. Considering the margin of error, is it possible that Crane will end up with half of the votes?

 31. If 400,000 votes were cast for these four candidates, *approximately* how many were cast for Crane?

32. Given the margin of error in this poll, is it possible that Davidson will win the election?

For problems 33–35, refer to the following data.

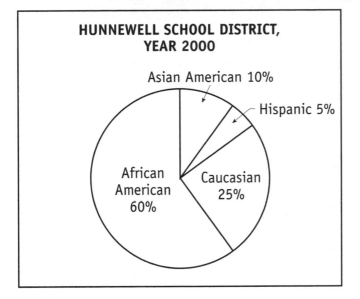

HUNNEWELL SCHOOL DISTRICT, YEAR 2000

Asian American 10%

Hispanic 5%

African American 60%

Caucasian 25%

33. What are the chances that a child in the Hunnewell School District is African American?

34. Write a statement comparing two racial groups in the Hunnewell School District in 2000.

35. If there are 12,400 students in the Hunnewell District in 2000, how many are Hispanic?

Posttest A Prescriptions

Circle the number of any problem that you miss. A passing score is 30 correct answers. If you passed the test, go on to Using Number Power. If you did not pass the test, review the chapters in this book or refer to these practice pages in other materials from Contemporary Books.

PROBLEM NUMBERS	PRESCRIPTION MATERIALS	PRACTICE PAGES
1, 2, 3, 6, 14, 17, 21, 34	understanding data	8–25
	Math Exercises: Data Analysis & Probability	3–5
	Math Problem Solver	160–167
4, 5, 7, 12, 13, 15, 18, 35	organizing data	28–59
	Math Exercises: Data Analysis & Probability	10–17
	Real Numbers: Tables, Graphs, & Data Interpretation	12–43
	Math Problem Solver	210–230
8, 9, 23, 24, 25, 28	evaluating data	114–141
10, 11, 29, 30, 32, 33	using probability and statistics	92–111
	Math Exercises: Data Analysis & Probability	20–26
16, 19, 20, 22, 26, 27, 31	using data sources	78–85
	Math Exercises: Data Analysis & Probability	8–9, 18–19, 25–26

For further data analysis practice:

Pre-GED/Basic Skills Interactive (software)
Mathematics Units 6, 7, and 8

GED Interactive (software)
Mathematics Units 4 and 5

Math Solutions (software)
Percents, Ratios, Proportions; Graphic Data

Posttest B

This test has a multiple-choice format much like the GED and other standardized tests. Take your time and work each problem carefully. Circle the correct answer to each problem. When you finish, check your answers at the back of the book.

For problems 1–4, refer to the following graphs.

HOMES BUILT IN WESTCHESTER COUNTY 1993–1998

1. How many homes were built in Westchester County in 1995?

   a. 150 **c.** 100
   b. 125 **d.** 75

2. Which statement best summarizes the data of both graphs?

   a. The size of the average home in Westchester County increased from 1993 to 1998.
   b. The number of homes built in Westchester County increased between 1993 and 1998.
   c. The number of homes in Westchester County decreased between 1993 and 1998.
   d. As the number of homes built in Westchester County increased between 1993 and 1998, the size of the average home increased.

SIZE OF AVERAGE HOME

3. Which statement best summarizes homes built in Westchester County in 1993?

   a. There were 50 homes built in Westchester County in 1993.
   b. There were fewer homes built in Westchester County in 1993 than in 1994.
   c. There were 50 homes built in Westchester County in 1993 with an average size of 550 square feet per home.
   d. The size of the average home in Westchester County in 1993 was 550 square feet.

4. Use data from both graphs to *estimate* how many square feet of homes were built in Westchester County in 1996.

   a. 6,000 **b.** 37,000 **c.** 37,500 **d.** 60,500 **e.** 262,500

For problems 5–6, refer to the following data.

5. Which of the following statements is true based on the data?

    a. There is a positive correlation between the amount of television watched and the number of correct answers on a standardized exam.
    b. There is no correlation between hours of television watched and correct answers on a standardized test.
    c. As the number of hours spent watching television per week increases, the number of correct answers on a standardized exam decreases.
    d. The greater the number of hours spent watching television, the higher the standardized test score.

6. Which of the following statements is true based on the data?

    a. There is a positive correlation between the number of hours spent reading and the number of correct answers on a standardized exam.
    b. There is no correlation between hours spent reading and correct answers on a standardized test.
    c. As the number of hours spent reading increases, the number of correct answers on a standardized exam decreases.
    d. The more hours spent watching television, the fewer hours spent reading.

For problems 7–10, refer to the following data.

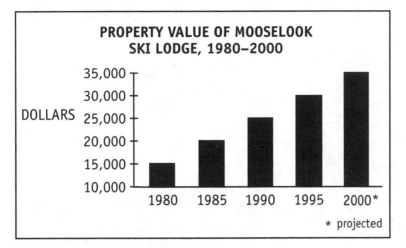

PROPERTY VALUE OF MOOSELOOK
SKI LODGE, 1980–2000

DOLLARS (y-axis: 10,000 / 15,000 / 20,000 / 25,000 / 30,000 / 35,000)

x-axis: 1980 1985 1990 1995 2000*

* projected

7. Which of the following statements is true according to the graph?

   a. The property value of Mooselook Ski Lodge increased by $10,000 every 5 years between 1980 and 2000.
   b. The property value of Mooselook Ski Lodge will exceed $40,000 in 2010.
   c. The property value of Mooselook Ski Lodge rose steadily between 1980 and 1995.
   d. The property value of Mooselook Ski Lodge decreased by $10,000 every 5 years from 1980 and 2000.
   e. The property value of Mooselook Ski Lodge decreased by $5,000 every 5 years between 1980 and 2000.

8. If the trend continues, what will the property value of Mooselook Ski Lodge be in 2005?

   a. $30,000   b. $40,000   c. $45,000   d. $50,000   e. $55,000

9. Which of the following statements is true based on the graph?

   a. The property value of Mooselook Ski Lodge in 1995 was twice as much as its value in 1985.
   b. The property value of Mooselook Ski Lodge in 1995 was half its value in 1985.
   c. The property value of Mooselook Ski Lodge in 2000 is expected to be more than twice its 1980 value.
   d. The property value of Mooselook Ski Lodge in 1980 was its lowest value ever.
   e. The property value of Mooselook Ski Lodge cannot be expected to exceed $40,000.

10. By what percent did the value of Mooselook Ski Lodge rise between 1980 and 1995?

    a. 100%   b. 75%   c. 50%   d. 25%   e. 10%

For problems 11–14, refer to the following data.

Projected North Dover High School PTO Budget, 2000	
Enrichment	41%
Field Trips	28%
Technology	22%
Guest Speakers	8%

Margin of error ± 3%

11. Given the margin of error, what is the range of percents of the projected budget for field trips in 2000?

    a. from 28% to 31%
    b. from 39% to 45%
    c. from 40% to 42%
    d. from 25% to 31%
    e. from 19% to 25%

12. Considering the margin of error, what is the greatest fraction of the budget that will be spent on technology in 2000?

    a. $\frac{1}{4}$ b. $\frac{1}{2}$ c. $\frac{1}{3}$ d. $\frac{1}{5}$ e. $\frac{1}{8}$

13. If the North Dover PTO spends $15,000 in 2000, how much will be spent on guest speakers?

    a. $120   b. $700   c. $1,875   d. $100   e. $1,200

14. Given the margin of error, what percent of the projected North Dover High School PTO budget will be spent on enrichment?

    a. 38%
    b. 41%
    c. between 38% and 44%
    d. between 39% and 46%
    e. 22%

For problems 15–17, refer to the following data.

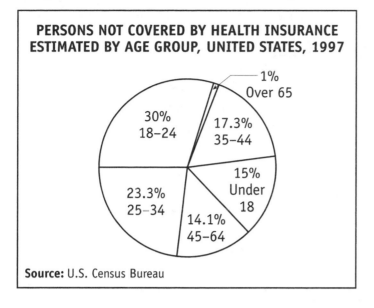

PERSONS NOT COVERED BY HEALTH INSURANCE
ESTIMATED BY AGE GROUP, UNITED STATES, 1997

1%
Over 65

30%
18–24

17.3%
35–44

23.3%
25–34

15%
Under
18

14.1%
45–64

Source: U.S. Census Bureau

15. Use data from the graph to *estimate* what the chances are that a
person not covered by health insurance in 1997 was between
25–34 years old.

  a. $\frac{3}{4}$ **b.** $\frac{2}{3}$ **c.** $\frac{1}{2}$ **d.** $\frac{1}{3}$ **e.** $\frac{1}{4}$

16. Which of the following statements is true based on the graph?

  a. Persons not covered by health insurance in 1997 were twice as
likely to be age 18–24 than under age 18.
  b. In 1997, 17.3% of persons in the United States who were not
covered by health insurance were 45–65 years old.
  c. Of persons in the United States, 30% were not covered by
health insurance in 1997.
  d. Of persons living in the United States, 50% were not covered by
health insurance in 1997.
  e. Persons not covered by health insurance in 1997 were three
times as likely to be age 18–24 than under age 18.

17. Which age group was most likely to be *covered* by health insurance
in the United States in 1997?

  a. 18–24   **b.** over 65   **c.** under 18   **d.** 45–65   **e.** 25–34

For problems 18–20, refer to the following data.

J. W. Eaton Elementary School

Grade	Number of Students Who Bring Their Lunch to School	Number of Students Who Buy Their Lunch	Total Number of Students
1	25	23	48
2	40	21	61
3	9	38	47
4	15	35	50
5	42	73	115

18. Which grade has the highest *rate* of students who bring their lunch to school?

    a. 1   **b.** 2   **c.** 3   **d.** 4   **e.** 5

19. According to the chart, about 60% of students at J. W. Eaton Elementary School buy their lunch. What number can you compare with this figure in order to decide if 60% is a large or a small number?

    a. the total number of students at J. W. Eaton Elementary School who bring their lunch
    b. the total number of students at J. W. Eaton Elementary School
    c. the percent of fifth graders who bring their lunch to school
    d. the percent of students who buy their lunch at a nearby elementary school
    e. the cost of an average lunch at J. W. Eaton Elementary School

20. Which of the following statements is true at the J. W. Eaton School?

    a. More fourth graders bring their lunch than buy their lunch.
    b. Almost $\frac{3}{4}$ of first graders buy their lunch.
    c. There are 50 students in the third grade.
    d. More than 50% of second graders buy their lunch.
    e. Of the fourth graders, 70% buy their lunch.

For problems 21–24, refer to the following data.

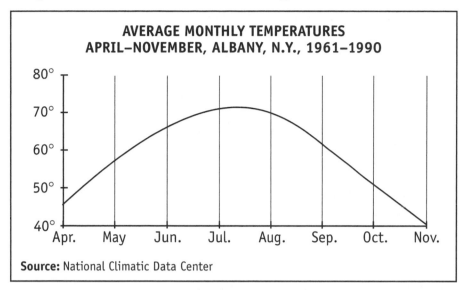

AVERAGE MONTHLY TEMPERATURES
APRIL–NOVEMBER, ALBANY, N.Y., 1961–1990

Source: National Climatic Data Center

21. Between what four months did the average monthly temperature rise in Albany, New York?

    a. August–November   c. July–October   e. April–July
    b. May–August   d. June–September

22. What is the range of temperatures provided on this graph?

    a. 40°–80°   b. 0°–80°   c. 30°–90°   d. 0°–40°   e. 30°–80°

23. Which of the following statements best summarizes the graph?

    a. The graph shows the monthly temperatures in Albany, New York, between April and November.
    b. The graph shows the average temperatures in Albany, New York, from 1961 to 1990.
    c. The graph shows the average monthly temperatures in Albany, New York, between April and November from 1961 to 1990.
    d. The graph shows the temperatures in Albany, New York.
    e. The graph shows the average monthly temperatures in the United States from 1961 to 1990.

24. According to the graph, which statement is true?

    a. The average monthly temperature in Albany, New York, in August was 70 degrees.
    b. The average monthly temperature in Albany, New York, fell between April and July.
    c. The average monthly temperature in Albany, New York, rose between July and November.
    d. The highest recorded temperature in Albany, New York, was 70 degrees.
    e. August is generally the hottest month in Albany, New York.

For problems 25–28, refer to the following survey.

A recent survey was conducted regarding eyeglasses and contact lenses wear. The results showed that 57% of visually impaired Americans own both contact lenses and glasses, 33% own only contact lenses, and 10% own only glasses. It was also found that 75% of those who own both contact lenses and glasses prefer to wear their contact lenses to their glasses.

25. Which of the following companies would most likely benefit from the statistics in the survey above?

    a. Tierney Eye Glass Wear, Inc.
    b. See Perfect Contact Lenses Manufacturers
    c. The Institute of Ophthalmology
    d. Pediatric Eye Associates
    e. Northeast Eye World

26. Which of the following questions might the surveyors ask to ensure that Americans who own both eyeglasses and contact lenses say they prefer wearing contact lenses to glasses?

    a. Which do you wear more often, contact lenses or glasses?
    b. Would you prefer to wear soft and comfortable contact lenses or your glasses?
    c. Which do you prefer to wear—glasses or contact lenses?
    d. Are your eyeglasses convenient to wear?
    e. Do you occasionally have trouble putting in your contact lenses?

27. Which of the following would be a biased sample on which to conduct the survey?

    a. 500 employees at a bank
    b. 1,000 people shopping at the mall
    c. 1,000 people walking out of a contact lenses fitting office
    d. 100 patients at an eye doctor's office
    e. 100 people at a county fair

28. According to the survey, what are the chances that an American wears only glasses?

    a. 1 out of 10   d. 1 out of 4
    b. 1 out of 5   e. 1 out of 20
    c. 1 out of 3

For problems 29–31, refer to the following data.

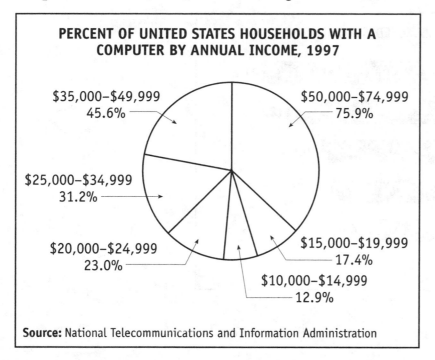

PERCENT OF UNITED STATES HOUSEHOLDS WITH A COMPUTER BY ANNUAL INCOME, 1997

$35,000–$49,999 45.6%

$50,000–$74,999 75.9%

$25,000–$34,999 31.2%

$20,000–$24,999 23.0%

$15,000–$19,999 17.4%

$10,000–$14,999 12.9%

Source: National Telecommunications and Information Administration

29. Which annual income group had the highest percent of households with a computer in 1997?

   a. $10,000–$14,999
   b. $35,000–$49,999
   c. $50,000–$74,999
   d. $15,000–$19,999
   e. $25,000–$34,999

30. What is the purpose of the graph above?

   a. to show how many households owned a computer in 1997
   b. to show which annual income group had the lowest and highest percent of households with a computer
   c. to show the percent of households with a computer by annual income in 1997
   d. to show the annual income of computer owners
   e. to show the rise in computer usage in the United States

31. Which of the following statements is false?

   a. Of the households with a computer in 1997, 75.9% had an annual income of $50,000–$74,999.
   b. In 1997, 12.9% of United States households had a computer.
   c. Households with a computer in 1997 were about twice as likely to have an annual income of $35,000–$49,999 than an annual income of $20,000–$24,999.
   d. Households with an income of $10,000–$14,999 were about half as likely to own a computer than households in the $20,000–$24,999 range.
   e. The higher the income, the more likely a household is to own a computer.

For problems 32–35, refer to the following data.

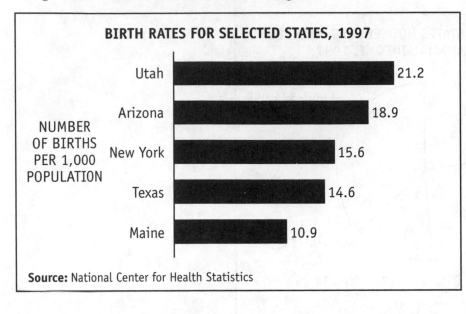

BIRTH RATES FOR SELECTED STATES, 1997

NUMBER OF BIRTHS PER 1,000 POPULATION

Utah 21.2
Arizona 18.9
New York 15.6
Texas 14.6
Maine 10.9

Source: National Center for Health Statistics

32. How many births per 1,000 population occurred in New York in 1997?

   a. 15.6 **b.** 1,560 **c.** 156 **d.** 100 **e.** 15.5

33. Which of the following statements summarizes the data?

   a. The graph shows the birth rate per 1,000 population in the United States.
   b. The graph shows the number of births that occurred in 1997 in five states.
   c. The graph shows the birth rates per 1,000 population for five states in 1997.
   d. The graph shows the population in four of the United States.
   e. The graph shows the rise in birth rates in the United States.

34. According to the chart, which of the following statements is true?

   a. Utah had the greatest number of births of the states listed.
   b. Of the states listed, Maine had fewer births per 1,000 population than any other state listed.
   c. In 1997 Arizona had more births per 1,000 population than Utah.
   d. More babies were born in New York than in Texas.
   e. The U.S. birth rate has declined since 1997.

35. According to the graph, which state had the highest rate of births per 1,000 population?

   a. Maine **b.** New York **c.** Arizona **d.** Utah **e.** Texas

Posttest B Chart

If you missed more than one problem on any group below, review the practice pages for those problems. Then redo the problems you got wrong before going on to Using Number Power. If you had a passing score, redo any problem you missed and go on to Using Number Power on page 167.

PROBLEM NUMBERS	SKILL AREA	PRACTICE PAGES
3, 16, 20, 23, 31	making statements about data	11–12
19	comparing numbers	16–18
18, 34	numbers vs. rates	22–24
22	scale and range	32–35
3, 21, 24	line graphs	38–42
32, 35	visual statistics	43
17, 29, 30	circle graphs	46–48
13, 33	using only the information given	70–72
4, 15	estimation	75–77
1, 2	using more than one data source	78–80
8, 9	seeing trends/making predictions	86–89
15, 28	using data to find probability	96–98
27	random samples	102–104
11, 12, 14	margin of error	109–111
10	zero on a scale	124–126
5, 6, 7	understanding correlation	127–131
25, 26	understanding bias	132–137

Using
Number
Power

A Look at the U.S. Census

Every 10 years, the federal government collects, tabulates, and publishes statistics about the American people. These statistics make up the **U.S. Census.** The census is used, among other things, to determine

- how many representatives each state should have in Congress

- how much money each city and state should receive in federal aid

- how much money to allocate for bilingual education

- the need for low-income housing

The census attempts to count *each and every person* living in the United States. Just imagine what a data collection task that is—considering that there are almost 270 million people living in the United States today! To get information from all these people, the government sends out questionnaires to home addresses. Those people who do not respond to the questionnaires are reached by door-to-door census takers. An estimated 315,000 civil servants were needed to collect and process the data for the 1990 census. Even more will be needed for the year 2000 census.

Because the census is such an enormous project, some people slip through the cracks and are not counted. This results in an *undercount*—a number below the actual total. Due to some serious undercounts in the 1990 census, efforts are currently being made to improve the accuracy of the year 2000 census.

What did the 1990 census tell us about the people of America? Here are some statistics.

Age
The nation's median age is 32.9 years. This is up from 30 years in 1980.

Sex
Of the population, 51% is female. This means that there are 6.2 million more women than men in the U.S.

Households

Of the U.S. households, 55% are maintained by married couples. This is down from the 1980 figure of 60%.

Persons living alone account for 25% of households.

Where We Live

Of the U.S. population, 77.5% lives in metropolitan areas.

The Los Angeles/Anaheim/Riverside metropolitan area experienced a 26% population growth, while the New York/New Jersey/Long Island/Connecticut area experienced a 3% growth.

The chart below contains some more data from the U.S. Census. Use the data to answer the following questions.

City	Official Population Count	Undercount
New York	7,322,564	3.0%
Los Angeles	3,485,398	5.1
Chicago	2,783,726	2.6
Houston	1,630,553	5.0

1. Which city has the highest official population count?

2. Which city has the highest percent of people who were not counted (undercounted) in the census?

3. **Critical Thinking**   Census data can be collected by mail, phone, and door-to-door interviews. Which person would be less likely to be counted: a homeless person or a homeowner? What effect do you think this has on the census statistics?

Are You Average?

As you know, comparing data is a good way to learn more about a subject. In this lesson, you will compare the amount of money you spend on certain items to the **average** expenditures among different groups in the United States. By doing this, you can learn *where you fall* among national averages.

First, estimate how much money you spend *per year* in the following categories.

To do this, multiply your *average* monthly expenditures by 12 or your *average* weekly expenditures by 52.

For example, if you spend about $50 per week on food,

$$\begin{array}{r} \$50 \\ \times\, 52 \\ \hline \$2{,}600 \end{array}$$

your *annual food expenditure* would be $2,600.

And if you spend about $30 per month on gas and oil for your car,

$$\begin{array}{r} \$30 \\ \times\, 12 \\ \hline \$360 \end{array}$$

your *annual gas/oil expenditure* would be $360.

Category	Annual Expenditure
Food, prepared at home	$_____ per year
Food, away from home	$_____ per year
Alcoholic beverages	$_____ per year
Clothing	$_____ per year
Gas and motor oil	$_____ per year

The chart below shows average expenditures in the United States by age, geographic region, and consumer unit. Circle the group that you belong in for each of the three categories: *age*, *region*, and *consumer unit*. Then answer the questions that follow.

Category	Food, Home	Food, Away	Alcoholic Beverages	Clothing	Gas and Motor Oil
Age					
Under 25	$1,121	$1,334	$312	$1,042	$ 659
25–34	2,046	1,618	355	1,504	923
35–44	2,599	2,037	281	2,015	1,152
45–54	2,605	2,210	307	2,112	1,248
55–64	2,355	1,597	239	1,355	970
65–74	1,933	1,081	162	977	729
75 and over	1,373	566	89	451	367
Region					
Northeast	$2,212	$1,781	$272	$1,619	$ 812
Midwest	2,084	1,577	273	1,465	893
South	2,039	1,514	229	1,406	1,025
West	2,282	1,643	326	1,521	952
Consumer Unit					
Buying for one person	$ 989	$1,099	$278	$ 893	$ 518
Buying for two or more people	2,585	1,813	265	1,722	1,093

Source: U.S. Census Bureau

1. Among people in your *age group*, do you spend more or less than the average on *food away from home?*

2. Among people in your *geographic region*, do you spend more or less than the average on *gas and oil?*

3. Write a statement comparing your *clothing* expenditures to the average in your *age group*. _____

    _____

4. Find a category in which your expenditures are far above or below the average in your age, region, or consumer unit size. Why do you think you are not close to the average? Write a short explanation.

    _____

Writing a Newspaper Article

In this activity, you will write articles and letters to the editor like those you see in the newspaper. Try to use as many of the techniques from the Analyzing Data chapter as you can, including

summarizing
estimating
using correct information
changing the form of data
seeing trends
making predictions

Also, try to use information from two or more of the data sources below in your article.

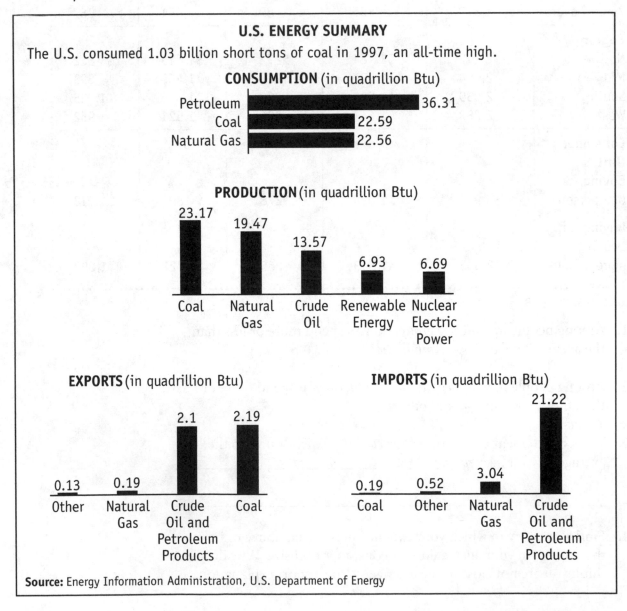

U.S. ENERGY SUMMARY

The U.S. consumed 1.03 billion short tons of coal in 1997, an all-time high.

CONSUMPTION (in quadrillion Btu)

Petroleum 36.31
Coal 22.59
Natural Gas 22.56

PRODUCTION (in quadrillion Btu)

Coal	Natural Gas	Crude Oil	Renewable Energy	Nuclear Electric Power
23.17	19.47	13.57	6.93	6.69

EXPORTS (in quadrillion Btu)

Other	Natural Gas	Crude Oil and Petroleum Products	Coal
0.13	0.19	2.1	2.19

IMPORTS (in quadrillion Btu)

Coal	Other	Natural Gas	Crude Oil and Petroleum Products
0.19	0.52	3.04	21.22

Source: Energy Information Administration, U.S. Department of Energy

1. Use one of the following statements for the first sentence in an article about our national energy situation. Write the article using any of the data from the previous page.

   a. The United States consumes most of the coal it produces.

   b. The United States consumes equal amounts of coal and natural gas.

   c. The United States exports more coal than it imports.

   _____

   _____

   _____

   _____

   _____

   _____

   _____

   _____

   _____

   _____

2. Do you have an opinion about our country's energy usage? For example, some people think that we are using up too much of our natural resources and that we should use more nuclear energy or renewable energy sources, such as solar or wind power. Other people believe that nuclear power is too dangerous and should not be used at all. Still other people believe that, no matter what our energy source is, we use too much of it on transportation, such as cars.

   On a separate sheet of paper, write a letter to the editor of a newspaper stating your opinion on energy in the United States. Use statistics to back up your point of view.

A Look at Political Polling in History

If you follow the news during election time in the United States, you are sure to be bombarded with statistics. For weeks before the election, you are showered with figures such as these.

- Candidate A is ahead of candidate B by 10%.

- Candidate C's name is recognized by 55% of the voting population.

- Candidate D rose 5% in the polls following a persuasive speech.

And now, with our rapidly improving technology, we even get up-to-the-hour statistics *as the election is taking place.* In **exit polls,** surveyors ask voters whom they voted for as they leave the polling site, and these figures are broadcast on television.

Now that you have a good understanding of samples and surveys, you know where these numbers come from. How reliable are these figures? The statistics you get from the major *independent* polling organizations (see pages 107–108) are generally very reliable. However, this was not always the case. Let's take a look at a famous case in which a survey provided very *unreliable* results.

President Thomas E. Dewey?

Polling and sampling techniques have improved greatly over the years. In the past, pollsters relied on a method of matching the U.S. Census exactly to get a representative sample. For example, if the census reported that 12% of the population was African American, pollsters made sure that 12% of their sample was African American. If 23% of the population commuted into a city to work, the sample had the same percentage.

Why, then, in 1948, did all three major national polls—Gallup, Roper, and Crossley—predict that Thomas Dewey would defeat incumbent Harry Truman? Truman won the election by a wide margin.

Many studies were done after this famous mishap. Looking back, we find that some mistakes were made in the surveying and sampling methods used by the polling organizations.

- The surveying took place weeks before the election. The surveys did not take into account a late trend favoring Truman.

- Pollsters were allowed to survey anyone they found in one area, while other areas and people weren't represented at all.

Since this embarrassing event, a great deal has been done to improve polling techniques. Surveys are now conducted right up to the day of an election. In addition, when surveyors are sent out to take a poll, they are given specific names and addresses of people to interview. These names are gathered by a true method of random sampling.

Basically, by putting the names of *every single American of voting age* on a list and choosing 1,200 of them at random, polling organizations ensure the principle of random sampling: *each member of the population is equally likely to be chosen.*

1. **Critical Thinking**   Very early in an election year, citizens find out who the front-runners are in a political race—based on public opinion polls. Even before we hear all of a candidate's points of view, we read about his or her chances of winning. Do you think public opinion polls have a good or bad influence on our political system?

Consider This Situation

A voter does some research on all of the candidates for office and decides he likes how Candidate X stands on almost all issues. The voter then learns—from early public opinion polls—that Candidate X is favored by only 10% of the population. Believing that his candidate does not stand a chance of winning, the voter decides to cast his vote for Candidate Y. He does this because he is strongly against Candidate Z and he believes that Candidate Y can defeat Candidate Z.

2. Do you think that early public opinion polls influence voters? Do they influence the outcome of an election? Do they serve a legitimate purpose in a democracy, or do they cloud the issues? Can you come up with arguments for and against such polls?

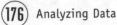

Numbers in Advertising

"4 out of 5 doctors surveyed recommend brand X!"

"Now a hot dog that's 80% fat-free!"

"Get your laundry up to 30% cleaner!"

Have you ever noticed how many advertisements use statistical claims?
Are these numbers facts, and should they persuade us to buy these products?

The skills you have been working on throughout this book also apply to analyzing data found in advertisements and commercials. For each of the claims above, let's look at the numbers and *what they really mean.*

> "4 out of 5 doctors surveyed recommend brand X!"

Ask yourself these questions.

- Can you tell how large a survey was conducted?

- Does the advertisement tell you what question was asked of the doctors in the survey?

The answers should make you question the claims being made.

Few, if any, advertisements will tell how the survey was conducted. Certainly, the makers of brand X would like you to believe that they surveyed thousands of doctors in a random sample and asked them what their favorite brand of pain reliever was. More likely, however, here is how they got their numbers:

They probably surveyed a small number of doctors, possibly doctors who work in their own research labs.

They most likely asked the doctors, "Would you recommend FeelGood pain reliever to your patients?" The doctors respond yes, but the advertisement does not say that they recommend ten other brands as well.

In fact, there is nothing *untruthful* in the advertisement. However, don't be fooled into assuming too much. When you see an advertisement like this one, think of not only what is being said but also what *isn't* being said. Remember what you have learned about source and bias!

> "Now a hot dog that's 80% fat-free!"

Many people see a label that says "80% fat-free" and think that a product is low in fat. But what it's really saying is that the product is 20% fat. That's $\frac{1}{5}$ of what you're about to eat.

Whenever you see a percent on a label or in an advertisement, try to restate the data so it's more specific and more meaningful.

> "Get your laundry up to 30% cleaner!"

Ask yourself, "30% cleaner than *what?*"

By not identifying what a product is being compared to, and by using impressive statistics, advertisements like this one can be misleading. Consumer beware!

1. **Critical Thinking**   What is a good way to decide what kind of medication to buy? Can advertisements really help you make a decision?

   Choose three or four advertisements that use statistics to help sell a product or service. They can be television commercials or newspaper or magazine ads.

   a. Write the exact statement that uses statistics.

   b. Then write one or two reasons why the statistics do *not* help you decide whether to buy the product advertised.

Answer Key

Pretest, pages 1–6

1. **b.** California. 32,000,000 is the largest number on the chart.

2. The table above shows the 1999 **population** to the nearest million for five states.

3. Answers may vary. A sample statement is given below.

   The 1999 population of Arkansas was about three quarters of the population of Alabama.

4. **c.** 28,000,000

	32,000,000	(California)
−	4,000,000	(Alabama)
	28,000,000	

5. **a.** 40%

6. being caught in traffic

7. Answers may vary. A sample statement is given below.

   About 50% of the people surveyed get angry at slow restaurant service.

8. 48%

   65% + 65% + 50% + 40% + 20% = 240%
   240 ÷ 5 = 48%

9. **b.** 85%

10. **c.** seven

    1990: about 70%
    1981: about 10%
    70 is seven times ten.

11. **c.** more than 90%

    The graph shows the percent rising, so the percent in 2000 will probably be greater than the 85% in 1998.

12. **b.** People rented more videotapes in 1998 than in 1997.

    Although more households had VCRs, you cannot assume that more videotapes were rented.

13.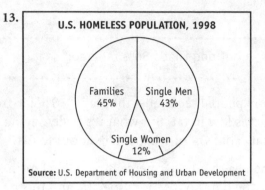

    U.S. HOMELESS POPULATION, 1998

    Families 45%
    Single Men 43%
    Single Women 12%

    Source: U.S. Department of Housing and Urban Development

14. **a.** 144

    12% of 1,200 is the same as 12% × 1,200, or 144.

15. Answers may vary. A sample statement is given below.

    More than three times as many single men as single women were homeless in the United States in 1998.

16. **c.** 3 out of 5

    $\frac{3}{5}$ (2, 6, and 10 are multiples of 2)
    (5 cards in all)

17. **a.** 0

    Since there are no fives, the probability of choosing a 5 is 0.

18.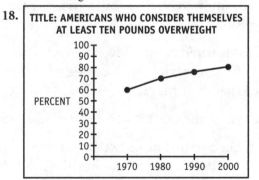

    TITLE: AMERICANS WHO CONSIDER THEMSELVES AT LEAST TEN POUNDS OVERWEIGHT

    PERCENT

    1970 1980 1990 2000

19. Answers may vary. A sample statement is given below.

    In general, as the age of the automobile increases, the number of repairs per year increases.

Page 10

Answers may vary.

Page 12

Answers may vary.

Pages 14 and 15

Yes	No	No Opinion
////	//	/

1. 95%, $\frac{95}{100}$; 95:100 or 19:20
2. 8%; $\frac{8}{100}$; 8:100 or 2:25
3. 70%; $\frac{7}{10}$; 7:10 or 70:100
4. 30%; $\frac{3}{10}$; 60:200 or 30:100 or 3:10
5. 1%; $\frac{1}{100}$; 1:100
6. 80%; $\frac{4}{5}$; 4:5 or 80:100

Pages 17–18

Answers may vary. Sample statements are given below.

1. $80,000 for the school lunch program would be a lot of money if **the total school budget was $100,000.**
2. $80,000 for the school lunch program would be a small amount of money if **$150,000 had been allotted for the program last year.**

Answers may vary. Here are some examples.

3. It would be helpful to know **how many people had been *expected* to attend.**
4. It would be helpful to know **how many people the company employs.**
5. It would be helpful to know **how many guns are confiscated in this area during a certain length of time.**
6. It would be helpful to know **how much money the artist usually gets for a painting.**
7. It would be helpful to know **how many years old the car is or how many miles it has on it.**

Pages 19 and 21

1. nine hundred thousand
2. eight million
3. ninety million
4. 100,000,000
5. 2,000,000,000
6. 700,000
7. 1,000
8. 10
9. 10
10. 100
11. 10

Pages 23–25

Highway

B	0.001	=	0.1	%
D	0.0033	=	0.33	%
G	0.0015	=	0.15	%
HH	0.0015	=	0.15	%
MM	0.002125	=	0.21	%

Answers may vary. Sample statements are given below.

1. Kramer, Inc., had the smallest number of satisfied employees, 13.
2. Psytech had the largest number of satisfied employees.
3. Psytech, with 11.5%, had the lowest satisfaction rate.
4. Horton & Co. had the highest satisfaction rate, almost 25%.
5. Although Psytech had the largest number of satisfied employees, its employee satisfaction rate was the lowest.
6. The unemployment rate decreased from 5.6% in 1995 to 4.5% in 1998.
7. Teenagers have a much higher unemployment rate than the total work force.
8. In 1995 the African American unemployment rate was more than twice that of Caucasians.

Pages 29–31

1. 1
2. 74
3. 152
4. T
5. T
6. T

Answers may vary. Sample statements are given below.

7. A one-ounce serving of peanuts **contains four more grams of fat than one ounce of potato chips.**
8. Although corn chips have more calories than potato chips, they contain less fat.
9. Answers may vary.

10.

Percent of Americans Holding Credit Cards

	$50,000 or More	$25,000–$34,999	Less than $15,000
Bank Credit Card	94%	73%	36%
Gasoline Credit Card	54%	33%	19%
Express Gold Card	14%	3%	1%

Source: *Money Express* magazine

11. 73

12. gasoline

13. $25,000–$34,999

14. 40

15. F

16. T

17. F

18. T

Answers may vary. Sample statements are given below.

19. The bank credit card **had the highest percent of credit card holders in every category.**

20. Americans earning less than $15,000 had the lowest percent of credit card holders.

Pages 33–35

1. 20%

2. 18%

3. 13%

4. 6%

5. Answers may vary.

6. Park and Recreation Land by County

7. counties

8. acres (in hundreds)

9. 0 to 20

10. 4

Answers may vary. Sample statements are given below.

11. Dawton County has more park and recreation land than **Kane County.**

12. Kane County **has less park and recreation land than the other counties shown.**

13. San Pedro County has the most park and recreation land of all the counties shown.

14.

Source: International Atomic Energy Agency

Answers may vary. Sample statements are given below.

15. In 1998 the United States had **more nuclear reactors than any of the other countries shown.**

16. Canada had **the same number of nuclear reactors as the Ukraine in 1998.**

17. France had **more than twice the number of nuclear reactors as Russia in 1998.**

Page 37

1. T

2. T

3. F

4. T

Page 39

1. 30 years old

2. 5 years

3. above

Answers may vary. Sample statements are given below.

4. The median U.S. age was the same in 1980 as it was in **1950.**

5. The median age in the United States rose steadily between 1820 and 1950.

6. The median age in the United States in 1990 was about 33 years old.

7. The baby boom was in the 1950s. Therefore, more babies were born, there were more younger people and that caused the median age to go down in the 1950s and 1960s.

Pages 41–42

1. risen
2. decreased
3. Saudi Arabia
4. United States
5. Saudi Arabia

6.

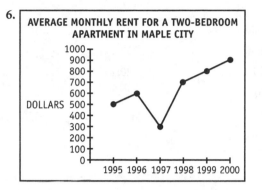

AVERAGE MONTHLY RENT FOR A TWO-BEDROOM APARTMENT IN MAPLE CITY

7. A line graph shows the change over time better than a bar graph.

Answers may vary. Sample statements are given below.

8. Rental prices in Maple City were about $600 higher in 2000 than in 1997.
9. Except for a sharp drop in 1997, rental prices rose between 1995 and 2000.

Page 43

Answers may vary. Sample statements are given below.

1. Between 1991 and 1997, poultry consumption in the United States **rose about 4 million pounds.**
2. Between 1994 and 1995, poultry consumption rose the least.

Pages 44–45

1. $50,000
2. 1995
3. 1997, $250,000
4. yes
5. $275,000

(**Note:** If you chose a different value in your key, your graph will be different from this one. Be sure that you have included the proper number of symbols on your graph.)

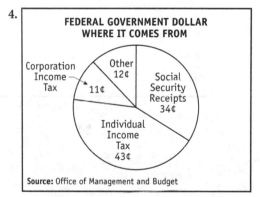

NORTH INVITATIONAL RACE TOTAL PRIZE MONEY

Key: 🚗 = $5,000

6–7. Answers may vary.

Pages 47–48

Answers may vary. Sample statements are given below.

1. There are fewer students from **the Middle East than from Asia.**
2. Students from Asia accounted for more than half of foreign students.
3. National defense receives about twice as much as states and localities.

4.

FEDERAL GOVERNMENT DOLLAR
WHERE IT COMES FROM

Corporation Income Tax 11¢

Other 12¢

Social Security Receipts 34¢

Individual Income Tax 43¢

Source: Office of Management and Budget

Answers may vary. Sample statements are given below.

5. More than half of federal money **comes from income taxes.**
6. Corporate income taxes bring in almost as much as other smaller sources combined.

Pages 49 and 51

1.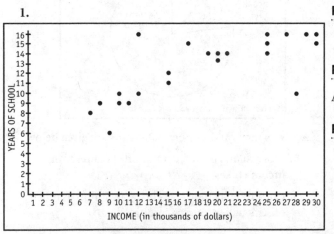

2. Two representatives is the least number from any state. Twelve states have two representatives.

3. California, with 52 representatives, has the greatest number. No other state has close to that many representatives.

4. There is a cluster of values between 2 and 12 representatives.

5. Answers may vary. Two sample statements are given below.

   a. Many states have **fairly small populations, and therefore only 2 to 4 representatives.**

   b. California has the largest population, and New York has the second largest.

6. Answers may vary.

Page 53

1.

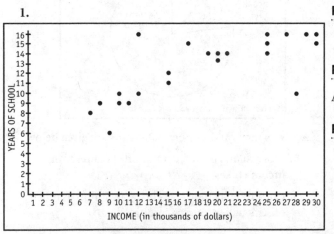

2. Yes, the higher the number of school years completed, the greater the salary.

Page 55

1. 4 miles

2. $70

3. $32

Page 56

1. $12.25

2. 6′10″

Page 57

1. 1,700:2   260:2
   1,650:1   250:9
   1,600:1   240:3
     290:2   230:1
     270:2   220:1

2. 250

3. $0.49

4. 10 weeks

Page 58

1. Mean: $646.67
   Median: $575
   Mode: $1,100
   Best representation of typical value: **mean or median**

2. Mean: 254 people
   Median: 200 people
   Mode: 225 people
   Best representation of typical value: **median or mode**

Page 59

1–2. Answers may vary.

Pages 60–61

Answers may vary.

Pages 65–66

1. No
   The *what* is inaccurate; the graph shows **different occupations,** not necessarily the best-paying jobs.

2. No
   The *where* is inaccurate; the graph shows the price of milk at **Crescent Farm Dairy.**

3. No
   The *what* and *how* are inaccurate; the chart shows Americans who **believe** it's all right to lie, **in percent,** not numbers.

4. Yes

Pages 68–69

1. The statement does not take into account the label (× 100) on the vertical axis; the number of passengers carried is 1,200, not 12.

2. The statement does not include the necessary time: 2000.

3. The statement does not tell what the 600 refers to; Carling Coach carried 600 passengers in 2000.

Answers may vary. Sample statements are given below.

4. According to the County Taxi Association, Carling Coach carried **half as many** passengers as Yellow Cab in 2000.

5. In 2000 At Your Service cab company carried **200 fewer passengers than** Yellow Cab, according to the County Taxi Association.

6. Yellow Cab carried **the greatest number of** passengers in 2000.

7. Speedy Taxi Co. carried $\frac{1}{3}$ **the number of passengers** than Yellow Cab in 2000.

Page 72

1. Just under half of people responding to the survey felt that safety from abuse is important. This does not mean that many children were victims.

2. The graph shows *percent* of people interviewed, not actual numbers—46%, not 46 people.

3. The graph describes people in Massachusetts, not the entire country.

Page 74

1. more than

2. between

3. almost, approximately

Answers may vary. Sample statements are given below.

4. The average annual cost of car insurance has risen steadily between 1990 and 2000.

5. The average annual cost of car insurance in 2005 is expected to be $1,400.

Page 77

1. In 2001 there will be **about** 7 million people between the ages of 70 and 74.

2. In 2001 there will be about **3** times as many women 40–44 years old than women 70–74 years old.

3. Of the 19 million children under 5 years old in 2001, **10 million** will be boys.

4. In 2001 there will be more than **4** times as many children under age 5 than men 70–74 years old.

5–6. Answers will vary.

Pages 79–80

1. Graph 2

2. Both

3. Neither

4. Graph 1

5. **a.** Chart
   b. $\frac{1}{10}$ ($\frac{140}{1,400} = \frac{1}{10}$)

6. **a.** Both
   b. 16 (20% of 80 = 16)

7. **a.** Graph
   b. 210 (15% of 1,400 = 210)

8. **a.** Neither
   b. The chart and graph give no information about which sexes participated in which activities.

Pages 83 and 85

1. 1996: 31%; 1999: 49%; 2000: 56%

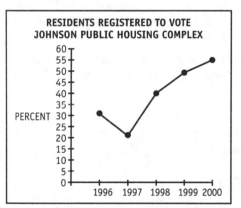

2. **a.** The *percent* of registered voters *rose* between 1999 and 2000, even though the first graph showed the *number* of registered voters falling.
   b. Answers may vary.

3. **Step 1.** 540
   Step 2. Medicare: 140 ÷ 540 = about 26%
   BC/BS: 120 ÷ 540 = about 22%
   Private: 200 ÷ 540 = about 37%
   No insurance: 80 ÷ 540 = about 15%
   Step 3.

Insurance	Medicare	Blue Cross/ Blue Shield	Private	No Insurance
Percent of Patients	26%	22%	37%	15%

4.

Sun County Homeless Population

Downtown Area	37% or 3,515
Central Square	29% or 2,755
East Side	22% or 2,090
West Side	10% or 950
Outlying	2% or 190

Pages 88–89

1. $900

Answers may vary. Sample statements are given below.

2. If the trend continues, the approximate monthly rent for a two-bedroom/two-bathroom apartment in Del County in 2001 will be $1,000.

3. **If the trend continues,** the number of PCs connected to the Internet in North America will be close to 50 million in 2002.

4. The number of PCs connected to the Internet in North America **rose steadily** between 1997 and 2000.

5. The number of PCs connected to the Internet in North America in 2001 **is projected to be** about 45 million.

6. There were **about 6 million fewer** PCs connected to the Internet in North America in 1998 than in 1999.

Page 91

Articles may vary.

Pages 92–93

1–3. Answers may vary. A sample statement is given below.

The total number of heads vs. the total number of tails is the same.

4. $\frac{1}{6}$

5. $\frac{3}{6}$ or $\frac{1}{2}$

6. $\frac{2}{6}$ or $\frac{1}{3}$

7. $\frac{9}{10}$

8. $\frac{1}{10}$

Pages 94–95

1. $\frac{1}{4}$ ← (number of fours)
   $\phantom{\frac{1}{4}}$ ← (total number of cards)

2. $\frac{3}{4}$ ← (4, 6, and 8 are greater than 3)
   $\phantom{\frac{3}{4}}$ ← (total number of cards)

3. $\frac{4}{4}$ or 1 (all numbers are divisible by 2)

4. 0 (none of the numbers is greater than 8)

5. Answers may vary.

6. 1

7. 1

8. Answers may vary.

9. 1

10. 0

11. 1

12. 1

13. 0

14. Answers may vary.

Answers may vary. Some examples are given below.

15. By the year 2000, animals will be able to talk as people do.
   A 3-year-old will be elected president in the next election.
   1 + 1 will no longer be equal to 2.

16. Someone in the world will make a new discovery this year.
   A baby will be born in this country this year.
   Some part of the earth will be in darkness today.

Pages 97–98

1. 44%

2. $\frac{44}{100} \approx \frac{40}{100} = \frac{2}{5}$

3. $\frac{2}{5}$

4. **Step 1.** 1,280 + 960 + 320 = 2,560
   Step 2. $\frac{1,280}{2,560} = \frac{1}{2}$

5. $\frac{5}{8}$ 7. less than $\frac{1}{2}$

6. $\frac{1}{8}$ 8. less than $\frac{1}{3}$

Page 101

1. Population: test scores of sixth-graders in state
   Sample: test scores of sixth-graders in six towns

2. Population: low-income people in city
   Sample: people in city low-income housing units

3. Population: defective canisters on early-morning shift

   Sample: defective canisters produced between 12:00 and 1:00 A.M.

4. Population: toy store's merchandise

   Sample: three toys from store

5. Population: all the baked goods in the store

   Sample: chocolate chunk cookies to passersby

Page 104

1. Population: Americans

   Sample: 200 people living near an army base
   The sample is not representative because people living near an army base may feel differently about defense than others.

2. Population: freshest food at the local market

   Sample: chickens in five different stores
   The sample is not representative of all food in the markets. Where chicken was fresh, produce, for example, may not have been; or vice versa.

3. Population: people of the United States

   Sample: members of American Small Business Owners Association
   The sample is not representative of Americans because it excludes all who do not own a small business.

4. Population: defective circuit boards each month

   Sample: first 100 circuit boards one Tuesday morning
   The sample is not representative because the Tuesday morning shift might be the best or worst shift of the week.

Pages 106–108

Answers should include some of the responses listed below.

1. Mail
   Advantages: inexpensive; can reach a wide and varied sample
   Disadvantages: low response rate; responses are often not representative of those who received the questionnaire

2. Telephone
   Advantages: accurate results because of good participation (more representative of population); easy to use
   Disadvantages: leaves out people without telephones; hard to verify information

3. Personal Interview
   Advantages: reliable; accurate; good participation (more representative of population)
   Disadvantages: expensive; often survey fewer people

4. Answers may vary.

Pages 109–111

1. 20%

2. 20% − 2% = 18%
   20% + 2% = 22%
   The range is from 18% to 22%.

3. The city council approval rating declined from March to April of 1999.

4. 60%

5. from 57% to 63%

6. 55%

7. from 52% to 58%

8. March: 57%
   April: 58%

9. Yes, when you consider the possible effect of the margin of error on the figures for both months

10. from 67% to 75%

11. Yes, it is possible.
    39% + 4% = a possible 43% who said they are happier
    46% − 4% = a possible 42% who said they are not happier
    39% ± 4% = 35% to 43% who said they are happier
    46% ± 4% = 42% to 50% who said they are not happier

12. 525 teenagers (35% of 1,500 = 525)

13. 105 teenagers (7% of 1,500)
    225 teenagers (15% of 1,500)
    150 teenagers (10% of 1,500)

Page 113

Survey questions may vary.

Page 115

1–3. Answers may vary.

Page 118–119

Answers may vary. The following are sample statements.

1. **a.** Although oral contraceptives have a low failure rate in preventing pregnancy, this does not make them the *best* method of birth control. Other factors such as a woman's age, health, lifestyle, and preferences need to be considered, and what is best for one person is not necessarily best for everyone.
   b. Oral contraceptives have a failure rate of 6%, compared to a 16% failure rate for condoms and an 18% failure rate for diaphragms.

2. **a.** Although North County pays higher police salaries than the other four counties, the salaries might not be *too* high. Maybe North County requires more skills among its police force, or perhaps the other counties' police salaries are too low.
   b. Full-time North County police officers were paid an average of $30,000 per year, the highest salary among the five counties listed.

3. **a.** Fire deaths in Massachusetts are not necessarily caused by poor fire protection. More fatal fires may occur in Massachusetts because of careless smoking, more frequent use of chemicals, more flammable building materials, and so forth.
   b. In the state of Massachusetts, 29 percent of fire deaths are caused by careless smoking.

Page 123

1. **a.** Statement 1 refers to Graph A.
   b. Statement 2 refers to Graph B.

2. Answers may vary. A sample statement is given below.

   According to Graph A, the population in Harris County was approximately 40,000, while in Drake County it was about 70,000.

3. **a.** Yes
   b. No

4. Answers may vary. A sample statement is given below.

   In Graph A the scale increases by 10,000. In Graph B the scale increases by 50,000. Because the spacing between 0 and 7 on Graph A is wider than the spacing between 0 and 7 on Graph B, the bars on Graph A are longer.

Page 126

1. The statement is not accurate because there is no zero on the scale. The bar for West Virginia is almost twice as long as the bar for Rhode Island, but the actual birthrates are in thousands.

2.

3.

Pages 129 and 131

1. Answers may vary.

2. **a.** There **is** a correlation between **monthly take-home pay** and **number of television sets owned.**
   b. The analysis is not accurate. Although there is a correlation, an increase in one value does not *cause* an increase in the other.

3. **a.** As the number of school years completed **rises,** the number of hours spent reading per week **rises.** (*Decreases* may also be used in both blanks.)
   b. There is a **positive** correlation between school years completed and time spent reading.

Pages 133, and 135–137

1. Answers may vary.

2. **Biased.** The group Citizens for Smith has an interest in more people voting for Smith.

3. **Biased.** A soft-drink company would want more teenagers to prefer its brand.

4. **Biased.** A group called Americans Tough on Criminals would most likely want to find large numbers of people in favor of capital punishment.

5. **Unbiased.** A newspaper would probably have no preference concerning how people feel about gun control.

6. **Biased.** A person trying to get financial support would most likely want to find a large number of people interested in his or her idea.

7. **Unbiased.** A television network generally shows no preference for a particular candidate.

8. In general, answers are yes.

9. **Biased.** The question asked is loaded. It emphasizes the advantages of a new factory without mentioning the possible disadvantages.

10. **Unbiased.** The network is most likely looking for facts and has no preference as to how the numbers turn out.

11. **Biased.** This question points out the disadvantages without mentioning the disadvantages.

12. **Biased.** The sample surveyed is not representative of Americans in general. People shopping at an exclusive shopping mall are not likely to be affected by a recession in the same way as other Americans.

13. **Biased.** People leaving an ice cream shop are more likely to prefer ice cream than the general population.

Page 141

1. Answers may vary. A sample statement is given below.

   In 1990 and 1991, there were more youth homicides by firearm than other years in the 1990s.

2. **a.** No youths were killed by firearm in Boston through March of 1999.

Page 143

Questionnaires will vary.

Posttest A, pages 144–153

1. service
   sales: $26 \div 110 \approx 0.24$
   service: $10 \div 25 = 0.4$

2. **b.** the percent of people who carpool to other nearby industries

3. Answers will vary. The following is a sample statement.

   The maintenance department has 10 times as many employees who carpool to work as management does.

4. **a.** The graph shows new one-family house sales in the U.S. from 1994 to 1999 in thousands of units.

5. from 400,000 to 1,000,000 units

6. Answers will vary. The following is a sample statement.

   One-family house sales in January 97 were about the same as in July 97.

7. **c.** January 1995 was the month in which the fewest new one-family homes were sold in the U.S. between 1994 and 1999.

   The number of new one-family homes was actually lower between January and April 1995.

8. **c.** American Potato Growers, Inc.

9. **a.** Would you prefer a hot, buttered baked potato or a bowl of rice?

10. **c.** 3,000 participants at the Potato Lovers Picnic

11. 1 out of 5 or $\frac{1}{5}$

12. cold beverages in cans

13. **c.** to show percentage of vending machine sales for different categories

14. Answers will vary. The following is a sample statement.

    Cigarettes had the least percentage of sales.

15. 1,228,000 workers

16. **c.** The graph shows the number of workers who worked at home between 1960 and 1990.

17. Answers will vary. The following is a sample statement.

    In 1960 the number of workers who worked at home were more than twice as many as in 1970.

18. **c.** In 1960 more workers worked at home than in an office or place of business.

    The graph shows workers who worked at home. You do not know how many workers worked in an office or place of business.

19. 11%

20. **b.** The percentage of Caucasians in the U.S. is projected to decrease, while the percentages of minorities will increase.
    The statements in both **a.** and **c.** are false.

21. Answers will vary. The following is a sample statement.

    By 2050 about half of the population will be Caucasian, while the other half of the population will be made up of minorities.

22. 13%

    There were about 12% African Americans in 1997, and 14% projected for the year 2050. Therefore, **13%** would be a good estimate of the African American population in 2020.

23. Yes

    As the number of leisure hours rises, the number of medicines taken also rises.

24. positive correlation

    As age increases, so does the number of medicines taken per year.

25. Answers will vary. The following is a sample summary.

    As age increases, so do the number of leisure hours and the number of medicines taken. Of these three factors, age is probably the one that has an effect on the other two. Older people tend to be retired, thus having more leisure time. In addition, older people tend to have more medical problems (high blood pressure, arthritis, and so forth) that may require medication.

26. Answers will vary. The following is a sample statement.

    The average monthly Calereso commission is projected to be $1,900 in 2000.

27. c. The average monthly commission at Calereso rose steadily between 1997 and 1999.
    The 1998 commission is *not* twice the 1997 commission. The graph appears that way because it does not have a zero on the vertical scale.
    The year 2001 is not shown on the graph.

28. The 1999 average monthly commission is *not* twice the amount earned in 1997. It appears that way on the graph because there is no zero on the vertical scale.

29. from 6% to 14%
    $10\% - 4\% = 6\%$
    $10\% + 4\% = 14\%$

30. Yes
    $46\% + 4\% = 50\% = \frac{1}{2}$

31. 200,000 votes
    46% is approximately 50%
    50% of 400,000 = 200,000

32. Yes
    If Crane actually received 46% – 4%, or 42%, and Davidson received 39% + 4%, or 43%, Davidson would be the winner.

33. $\frac{3}{5}$
    $60\% = \frac{60}{100} = \frac{3}{5}$

34. Answers will vary. The following is a sample statement.

    Hispanics in Hunnewell schools make up 5% of the school population, about half the Asian American population.

35. 620 students
    5% of 12,400 = $0.05 \times 12,400 = 620$

Posttest B, Pages 155–164

1. c. 100

2. d. As the number of homes built in Westchester County increased between 1993 and 1998, the size of the average home increased.

3. c. There were 50 homes built in Westchester County in 1993 with an average size of 550 square feet per home.

4. e. 262,500
   There were about 125 homes built in 1996, with an average size of about 2,100 square feet.
   $125 \times 2,100 = 262,500$

5. c. As the number of hours spent watching TV per week increases, the number of correct answers on a standardized test decreases.

6. a. There is a positive correlation between the number of hours spent reading and the number of correct answers on a standardized exam.

7. c. The property value of Mooselook Ski Lodge rose steadily between 1980 and 1995.
   The property value of Mooselook Ski Lodge increased by $5,000 every 5 years.
   The year 2010 is not shown on the graph.

8. b. $40,000
   $35,000 + $5,000 = $40,000

9. c. The property value of Mooselook Ski Lodge in 2000 is expected to be more than twice its 1980 value.
   The property value of Mooselook Ski Lodge in 1995 was not twice as much as it was in 1985.
   The graph appears that way because it does not have a zero on the vertical scale.

10. a. 100%
    $15,000 increased to $30,000 is a 100% increase.

11. **d.** from 25% to 31%
    28% − 3% = 25%
    28% + 3% = 31%

12. **a.** $\frac{1}{4}$
    22% + 3% = 25% = $\frac{1}{4}$

13. **e.** $1,200
    8% of $15,000 = 0.08 × $15,000 = $1,200

14. **c.** between 38% and 44%

15. **e.** $\frac{1}{4}$
    23.3% is approximately 25%.
    25% = $\frac{25}{100}$ = $\frac{1}{4}$

16. **a.** Persons not covered by health insurance in 1997 were twice as likely to be age 18–24 than under age 18.

17. **b.** over 65

18. **b.** 2(40 ÷ 61 = 0.66)

19. **d.** The percent of students who buy their lunch at a nearby elementary school.

20. **e.** Of the fourth graders, 70% buy their lunch.
    $\frac{35}{50}$ = $\frac{70}{100}$ = 70%

21. **e.** April–July

22. **a.** 40°–80°

23. **c.** The graph shows the average monthly temperatures in Albany, New York, between April and November from 1961 to 1990.

24. **a.** The average monthly temperature in Albany, New York, in August was 70 degrees.

25. **b.** See Perfect Contact Lenses Manufacturers

26. **b.** Would you prefer to wear soft and comfortable contact lenses or your glasses?

27. **c.** 1,000 people walking out of a contact lenses fitting office

28. **a.** 1 out of 10

29. **c.** $50,000–$74,999

30. **c.** to show the percent of households with a computer by annual income in 1997

31. **b.** In 1997, 12.9% of United States households had a computer.
    In 1997, 12.9% of United States households with a computer had an annual income of $10,000–$14,999.

32. **a.** 15.6

33. **c.** The graph shows the birth rates per 1,000 population for five states in 1997.

34. **b.** Maine had fewer births per 1,000 population than any other state listed.

35. **d.** Utah

Page 169

1. New York has the highest official population count.

2. Los Angeles has the highest percent of people who weren't counted.

3. A homeless person (or people living in shelters) would less likely be counted in census data. Therefore, the statistics would be lower than the actual population.

Page 171

1–4. Answers may vary.

Page 173

1–2. Answers may vary.

Page 175

1–2. Answers may vary.

Page 177

1. **a.** Statements will vary depending on the statistics used in the advertisements.
   b. Reasons will vary.

Using a Calculator

A calculator is a useful tool when you are working with graphs and data. It can perform complex operations quickly, easily, and accurately. The data from a graph can be input into a calculator to find even more values.

COLLEGE CREDIT

A national random sample of 750 college students found that credit card use is a reality for today's students.

HOW MANY CARDS DO YOU OWN?

Of all survey respondents

None 36%

1–3 50%

4 or more 14%

Source: *Boston Globe,* August 1999

EXAMPLE　The graph above is based on a national random survey of 750 college students. Of those students, how many do *not* own any credit cards?

What is 36% of 750? Use a calculator to find out.

Press Keys	Display Reads
. 3 6	0.36
×	0.36
7 5 0	750.
=	270.

You have used the data shown on the graph as well as your calculator to determine that 270 out of 750 college students do *not* own any credit cards. When you use a calculator, keep the following in mind.

- Enter numbers and operations carefully; watch the display to be sure you have entered the numbers you want.

- Check your calculations by repeating them, or by performing the opposite operation.

- Your thinking skills are as important as your calculator skills. Don't cut back on study time thinking that your calculator will guarantee success!

Using Mental Math

Reading graphs and data can sometimes be as easy as using your head. You can often interpret numbers simply by combining your own common sense and your understanding of data and graphs.

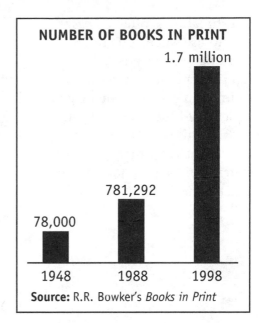

NUMBER OF BOOKS IN PRINT

1.7 million

781,292

78,000

1948   1988   1998

Source: R.R. Bowker's *Books in Print*

EXAMPLE   About how many times as many books were in print in 1988 than in 1948?

To solve this problem, use your thinking skills.

How does 781,292 compare to 78,000?

Try comparing the number of digits in each amount. There are six digits in one number and five in the other. Can you see that this one digit means that one number is 10 times the other?

Without doing any pencil and paper or calculator work, you can use your mental math skills to find that in 1988 there were about 10 times as many books in print as in 1948.

Doing calculations in your head can save time and energy. However, mental math skills take a while to develop. Get plenty of practice using this skill and always check your answers!

Using Estimation

Estimating is often an easy skill to use when you are working with graphs. Why? Graphs lend themselves to estimation because you are given a picture of the data, and you can use this picture to draw conclusions and make statements that do not involve exact values.

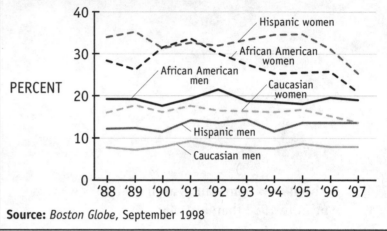

YOUNG ADULTS (16 TO 24) OUT OF SCHOOL, OUT OF WORK

When young adults are neither employed nor in school, there is concern about their status and activities as well as their future earnings prospects. Women in this situation may be raising children.

Source: *Boston Globe*, September 1998

EXAMPLE 1 Approximately what percent of Caucasian women ages 16–24 were out of school and out of work in 1997?

ANSWER: Find the light colored dotted line that indicates Caucasian women. Where does that line fall in 1997? As you can see, it is nearest to the 15% line. 15% is a good estimate.

EXAMPLE 2 In what two years was the percent of out of work, out of school Hispanic women the same as African American women?

ANSWER: Find the two places where the dotted lines for Hispanic women and African American women cross. Can you see that during the years 1990 and 1991, the values are the same?

Remember that when you estimate, you are finding a value that is close to an exact value.

Measurements

Time

365 days = 1 year
12 months = 1 year
52 weeks = 1 year
7 days = 1 week
24 hours = 1 day
60 minutes = 1 hour
60 seconds = 1 minute

Length and Area

5,280 feet = 1 mile
1,760 yards = 1 mile
3 feet = 1 yard
36 inches = 1 yard
12 inches = 1 foot
144 square inches = 1 square foot
4,840 square yards = 1 acre
1,000 meters = 1 kilometer
100 centimeters = 1 meter
1,000 millimeters = 1 meter
10 millimeters = 1 centimeter

Weight

2,000 pounds = 1 ton
16 ounces = 1 pound
1,000 grams = 1 kilogram
1,000 milligrams = 1 gram

Volume

4 quarts = 1 gallon
2 pints = 1 quart
4 cups = 1 quart
2 cups = 1 pint
32 ounces = 1 quart
16 ounces = 1 pint
8 ounces = 1 cup
1,000 milliliters = 1 liter

Glossary

A

analyze   To study or examine closely

average   The middle value of a group of numbers. An average is found by adding a group of numbers and dividing the total by the number of items in the group.

Example: What is the average of these numbers: 35, 25, 48?
$35 + 25 + 48 = 108$ $108 \div 3 = \mathbf{36}$

axis   One of the straight lines, either vertical or horizontal, that run from bottom to top or left to right on a graph

B

bar graph   A visual picture of data that uses rectangles to represent number values

vertical data bars   horizontal data bars

bias   An attitude that always favors one way of thinking over another

C

chart   A visual representation of data that uses columns and rows to make numbers easier to interpret

circle graph   A visual representation of data that illustrates size or percent as pie-shaped parts of a circle

circle graph

column   A vertical arrangement of numbers

compare   To decide whether one number is equal to, less than, or greater than another number

Example: $3.7 > 3\frac{1}{2}$ (3.7 is greater than $3\frac{1}{2}$.)

conclusion

conclusion   A decision reached by critical thinking

convert   To change from one unit of measurement to another

Example: How many feet are there in 60 inches?
$60 \div 12$ (inches per foot) = **5 feet**

correlation   A mutual relationship between two things

D

data   A collection of numbers that gives information about something

decimal   A value less than 1 and written to the right of a decimal point

Example: 12.125 (0.125 is a decimal and is less than one.)

E

estimate   To find an approximate number, a number that is close to the actual value

An estimate for $597 + 101$ would be $600 + 100 = 700$.

equation   A mathematical statement that says two values are equal

Example: $3 + 8 = 11$ is an equation. $27 - x = 20$ is an equation.

expression   The use of math symbols to represent the relationship between numbers

Example: $x \div 25$ (x is being divided by 25)

F

fraction   A number less than 1, written as part over whole

Example: $\frac{3}{4}$ is a fraction (3 is the part; 4 is the whole)

friendly numbers   Numbers that are easy to work with

Example: 100 and 10 are friendly numbers because one divides easily into the other.

H

heading   A label that appears at the top of a graph or chart

horizontal   The direction from left to right

K

key   The part of a graph that provides an explanation or identification of symbols

L

label   The words used to identify what the numbers on a graph or chart refer to

line graph   A picture of data that uses lines or segments to connect numerical values

line graph

M

mean   Average value; the amount found by adding a group of numbers and dividing by the number of items in the group

median   The number in a series of numbers arranged from smallest to largest at which there is an equal number of values higher and lower

mode   The most frequently appearing value in a set of data

multistep problem   A problem that takes more than one operation to solve

O

order of operations   The acceptable order in which to perform math operations in a multistep problem

Example: In the problem $(5 + 4) \div 3$, you add the numbers in parentheses before you divide.

ordering   The process of putting numbers in order from least to greatest or greatest to least

P

percent   A whole that is divided into one hundred equal parts. % = percent

Example: 43% means 43 out of 100.

pictograph   A visual picture of data that represents values with small symbols

horizontal display

vertical display

place value   The position a digit holds in a number

Example: In 27,439, the 7 is in the thousands place.

prediction   A foretelling based on observation and analysis of data

probability   A measure of how often an event is likely to happen

process   A step-by-step method for completing a task

R

range   The variation between the lowest and highest values in a set of data

rate   A comparison of one number to another that does not change; a constant ratio

ratio   A comparison of one number to another

Example: 4/5, 4:5, and 4 to 5 are all ratios comparing 4 to 5.

rounding   Changing the value of a number slightly so that it ends in a number that is easy to work with

Example: 89 can be rounded to 90; 2.03 can be rounded to 2.

row   A horizontal arrangement of numbers

S

scale   The series of spaces on the axis of a graph that increase equally

set-up problem   A problem that does not require computation. Instead, it requires you to choose the correct method for solving a problem.

source   The place from which data is obtained

statistics   The collection, organization, and interpretation of data

survey   A scientific gathering of data

T

table   A chart of data that shows rows and columns of data

trend   A general direction that shows a consistent pattern

V

vertical   The direction from top to bottom

W

word problem   A math problem that asks a question in words

Index

A

Advertising 176
Average (see *mean*) 170

C

Calculator 190
Charts 28
Critical thinking 59, 138

D

Data 8
    analyzing 62
    drawing conclusions 116
    evaluating 114
    forms 81
    gathering 9, 26
    organizing 28, 60
    projections 88
    reading 67, 70
    sources 64, 78
    summarizing 90

E

Estimation 73, 75, 192

G

Graphs
    bar graph 32
    circle graph 46
    double bar graph 36
    horizontal axis 32
    importance of zero 124
    line graph 38, 40
    misinterpreting 120
    pictograph 44
    range 32
    scale 32
    vertical axis 32
    zero break 125

L

Line plot 49, 61

M

Margin of error 109
Mean (average) 54, 58
Median 56, 58
Mental math 191
Mode 57, 58

P

Polls (see *surveys*) 174
Predictions, making 86
Probability 92
    between 1 and 0 94
    using data 96

R

Rates 22

S

Sampling 99
    random 102
Scatter diagram 52
    cause 129
    negative correlation 128
    positive correlation 127
Statistics 13, 43
    bias 132, 134, 135
Surveys (polls) 105, 112, 142
    bias 132, 134, 135

T

Tables 28
Trends, seeing 86, 87

U

U.S. Census 168